PRAISE FOR
"BEYOND EMPLOYEE ENGAGEMENT"

"This book is a great overview of the entire employee journey designed to make every person in your organization feel seen, heard and loved. It has practical "try this" ideas in each and every chapter and you're likely to learn something new from the perspective of all of your stakeholders, especially the HR function, from whom we don't often hear. Make this your book to read this year."

Dr. Louise Lambert
Editor of the Middle East Journal of Positive Psychology

"Kristina's candid narrative about her personal workplace anecdotes makes her book an engaging and relatable read, especially resonating with HR professionals seeking insights into enhancing the workplace experience."

Florencio, Jr. 'Rhency' Padilla
Founder/Managing Director, Perky People

"Packed with real-life, actionable examples and innovative ideas, "Beyond Employee Engagement" is every Leader's handbook when it comes to bolstering the employee experience from beginning to end. Whether you are just starting out as a Manager, or you're a CEO, "Beyond Employee Engagement" will give you the tools to empower your people, while directly impacting your customer experience and ultimately, your business profitability."

Rachael Knowles
Internal Communication Manager, Hospitality Industry

"Beyond Employee Engagement: Building workplace cultures that drive legendary employee experiences and phenomenal customer experiences", by Kristina Vaneva, is a must-read for leaders at any level in the business who would like to transform their organization and release the power of all employees to truly delight their customers. Kristina draws on her extensive experience working for and consulting with world-class organizations along with a robust academic pedigree to provide the reader with practical and proven strategies for building a culture where employees are not only engaged but also empowered, motivated, and committed to delivering results. She demonstrates how to foster a sense of purpose, trust, and ownership among employees and how to align their goals with the vision and values of the organization. She also shares real-life examples and case studies of successful companies that have implemented her approach and achieved remarkable outcomes. There are also great examples of what not to do or what to avoid. This book is full of valuable insights and actionable advice that will help you take your leadership and your organization to the next level. I highly recommend it to anyone who wants to create a high-performance culture that drives business success."

Gerard Moss
Senior HR Leader, Hospitality Industry

"One hundred and twenty years ago, George Bernard Shaw wrote that those who can, do; and those who cannot do, teach. 120 years ago, they had no Kristina Vaneva. Kristina can, she does, and she teaches others how to do it. A veritable antithesis to GBS's dictum.

We have all become somewhat familiar with the concept of Ikigai in our personal lives. Over the years, Kristina has mastered its equivalent for corporations and organizations—Employee Engagement. You could call it the secret sauce of success and, in this book, she shares her recipe."

Ambrose Muscat
MLRO & Compliance Manager, E-Sports Entertainment Group

"This book is a captivating journey through toxic workplaces to discovering a passion for employee experience. Kristina's emphasis on wellness and the powerful line, 'I learned then that if I didn't make time for my wellness, I'd be forced to make time for my illness,' struck a deep chord.

The unique perspective on career building, not solely based on experience but on attitude and cultural fit, challenges conventional narratives. The introduction promises a definitive blueprint for legendary workplace cultures, making it a valuable read for those navigating early career complexities and seeking inspiration and authenticity!"

Taniya Khadri
Paralegal

"In this transformative book, Kristina illuminates how every touchpoint shapes not just employee satisfaction but the very experience our customers receive. Reading it taught me how to unlock the key to inspiring our workforce and providing unparalleled customer service.

This isn't just dry theory; "Beyond Employee Engagement" is forged from the author's passionate heart, drawing on her personal journey, invaluable experiences, and years of meticulous research. It's an arsenal of actionable insights and practical strategies that can be readily implemented in any organization of any size or industry.

Imagine a workplace where your employees are motivated, engaged, and constantly striving to deliver exceptional customer experiences. That's the power you unlock with "Beyond Employee Engagement". This book is more than valuable; it's essential for anyone wanting to build a thriving organization where employees and customers sing its praises.

Don't settle for mediocrity. Seize the opportunity to transform your workplace and unleash its full potential."

Mounaim Lamouni
Assistant Vice President—Culture and Engagement,
Aldar Properties

BEYOND EMPLOYEE ENGAGEMENT

KRISTINA G. VANEVA

PASSIONPRENEUR®
PUBLISHING

BEYOND EMPLOYEE ENGAGEMENT

The definitive blueprint for building legendary workplace cultures that drive outstanding employee experiences and phenomenal customer experiences!

KRISTINA G. VANEVA

PASSIONPRENEUR®
PUBLISHING

Beyond Employee Engagement
Copyright © 2024 Kristina G. Vaneva
First published in 2024

Print: 978-1-76124-146-8
E-book: 978-1-76124-148-2
Hardback: 978-1-76124-147-5

Because of the dynamic nature of the Internet, any web addresses or links contained in this book may have changed since publication and may no longer be valid. The information in this book is based on the author's experiences and opinions. The views expressed in this book are solely those of the author and do not necessarily reflect the views of the publisher; the publisher hereby disclaims any responsibility for them.

The author of this book does not dispense any form of medical, legal, financial, or technical advice either directly or indirectly. The intent of the author is solely to provide information of a general nature to help you in your quest for personal development and growth. In the event you use any of the information in this book, the author and the publisher assume no responsibility for your actions. If any form of expert assistance is required, the services of a competent professional should be sought.

Publishing information
Publishing and design facilitated by Passionpreneur Publishing
A division of Passionpreneur Organization Pty Ltd
ABN: 48640637529

Melbourne, VIC | Australia
www.passionpreneurpublishing.com

To my wonderful family.
I am eternally grateful for your endless love and support.

TABLE OF CONTENTS

PART 1: A LEGENDARY EXPERIENCE

PART 5: SHUKRAN, CIAO AND AU REVOIR

FOREWORD

**By Dave Ulrich, Rensis Likert Professor,
Ross School of Business, University of Michigan**

Twenty-four hours in a day, 168 hours in a week. What percentage of that time do you spend at work, going to/from work, and thinking about work? For many of us, work-related activities form a large portion of our waking hours (and sometimes impact sleep time!). In today's work world, employee experiences become a lead indicator of customer and investor experiences. As customers, we have all experienced both positive and negative employee experiences that shaped our attitude not only about the employee, but also the organization. Employee experiences drive customer experiences leading to investor experiences that make up the overall experience economy.

Even more, what happens at work very likely does not just stay at work. Our work experiences influence our personal lives with family and friends. A good or bad day at work will often determine how we feel about non-work activities. In a hybrid, more fluid work world, boundaries between work and non-work activities increasingly blur.

Kristina takes us on her journey of learning about and creating employee experiences for herself and others. She weaves together insights from others and her personal stories to offer specific guidance and actions on how any individual can create a more positive personal work experience and how HR and business leaders can drive organization-wide employee experience.

Integrating others' research and her experiences, she offers specific tips for how to improve the employee experience in both the physical/technological environment and the social/cultural environment. She demonstrates how the systems and processes (culture, staffing, communication, rewards and recognition, celebration, job and work design, learning and development, exiting a company, and analytics) can be designed to institutionalize engagement. Each chapter integrates relevant ideas, offers tools, and then suggests actions for making engagement happen.

In our book "Why of Work", we identified seven factors that created an "abundant" organization where people are engaged. Since then, we have distilled these factors into four themes:

Be Safe

1. I have a job because my organization will succeed
2. Strengthen safety and healthy living
3. Promote a healthy work environment

Believe

1. Clarify beliefs, values, desires
2. Connect work to my values, causes, people
3. Connect work to organizational outcomes I believe in

Become
1. Develop and promote a growth mindset
2. Remember, "I'm not failing. I'm learning."
3. Take risks to grow

Belong
1. Connect with others by engaging
2. Connect by being authentic
3. Connect by supporting

Kristina's work moves "beyond" and enhances these ideas. What stands out for me is that her thoughtful ideas about employee engagement at work have an impact across boundaries. Thus, the title "beyond" employee engagement leads to engagement in personal, family, community, and non-work-related activities. We have all experienced moments of delight where we feel purposeful, passionate, and connected. And, we have experienced the opposite, where we feel drained, demoralized, and isolated. The insights, tips, and tools Kristina offers can be used for personal engagement at work and not at work, but also for creating a more engaged organization.

PART 1 A Legendary Experience

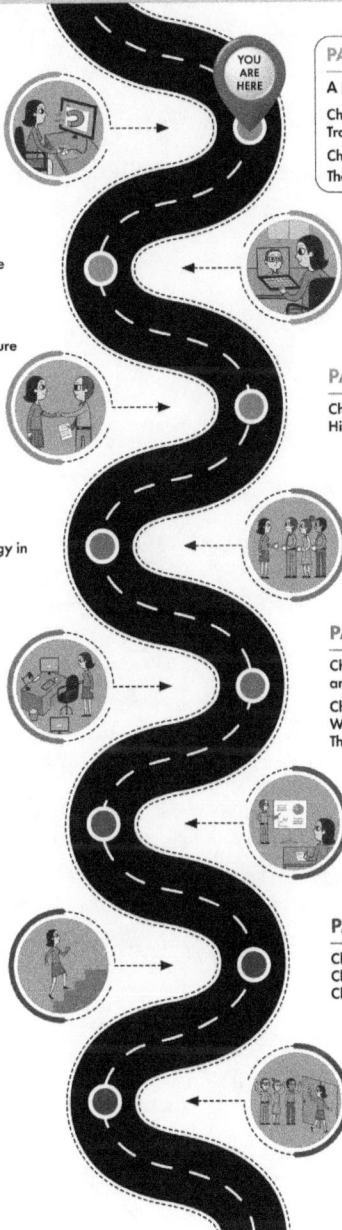

CHAPTER 1

THE JOURNEY OF TRANSFORMATION

In the summer of 2003, my grandfather passed away. I was not allowed to attend his funeral.

From that pivotal moment, I embarked on a journey that would shape how I view the world of work and, ultimately, the world itself. As I stood at that crossroads between duty and ambition, I made a choice that would set the course for a career dedicated to transforming workplaces into havens of inspiration and profound connection.

This journey began while I was living in Malta, a tiny group of islands in the Mediterranean Sea, working as a hostess in a popular nightclub. Meanwhile, my beloved grandfather was hospitalized in my native Bulgaria. Summer in Malta was the zenith of a pulsating and unforgettable clubbing scene, and my role required me to navigate this world independently, serving an exclusive clientele.

When my grandfather passed away, my boss presented me with an unfair dilemma. Attending his funeral would mean sacrificing my job—a job I had held for six years, where I was regarded as a loyal and invaluable team member. He warned me that if I traveled, I would not have a job when I came back. In essence, he strongly discouraged me from leaving the country.

This decision tore at my heartstrings. My grandparents had been my pillars since childhood, raising me alongside my parents in Libya and meaning the world to me. Still, my job also provided me with the financial independence I yearned for in my early twenties. The thought of getting fired was frightening, so I made the difficult choice not to attend the funeral. I should never have been asked to make that choice.

My journey through the world of work led to enriching experiences, from companies that disregarded work–life balance to roles that left me perpetually bored. In some companies, I worked eleven to thirteen hours daily for weeks without even a word of recognition. Elsewhere, I lacked a sense of direction, guidance, and motivation, spending most of my time surfing the internet. I had toxic bosses who created unbearable work conditions, so much so that I developed a dangerously overactive thyroid gland at one highly stressful workplace. During these trials, I learned a critical lesson: If I didn't make time for my wellness, I'd be forced to make time for my illness.

The harsh reality is that such workplaces exist across the globe, in every industry. In 2008, when I embarked on a new chapter in the United Arab Emirates, I made a solemn vow. I committed to creating workplaces that radiated happiness, engagement, and opportunities to flourish. Organizations where employees felt psychologically safe, inspired, and deeply connected to their work, leaders, and colleagues. Places where every individual knew they mattered and, as a result, delivered extraordinary customer experiences.

Throughout this journey, spanning over sixteen years of combined work experience at some of the largest organizations in the U.A.E., and as an independent workplace consultant, I've had the privilege of collaborating with approximately twelve thousand extraordinary individuals from over ninety diverse nationalities. When I first began my HR career at one of the largest resorts in the Middle East, I was hired based on my qualifications and work experience. I was also offered the opportunity because of my positive attitude, creative and resourceful mindset, and essentially because I was a culture fit and a culture build. I came to understand this later and learned the importance of hiring individuals who fit the culture in addition to people who can be instrumental in building a culture of brilliantly exceptional mindsets. These people are talents who can be encouraged to thrive, create, and show their true colors—not only for the benefit and growth of an inclusive and diverse organization, but also for the benefit of their customers, the UAE community, their home countries, and the world at large.

Starting anew in a foreign country, within an unfamiliar industry, and in a role I knew little about was initially daunting, but the strong leadership team and my intuition paved the way to a massively successful career. I achieved remarkable results, knowing that my endeavors genuinely improved the lives of thousands of employees and their families and left an indelible mark on the millions of customers we served. Together with my immediate team of committed superstars, and with the involvement of thousands of passionate volunteers and champions from other departments, we achieved transformational results. I pioneered the development and execution of the employee experience strategy and the employer branding plan, culminating in numerous prestigious local and international awards.

However, things were not very impressive to start with. We experienced a high employee turnover rate, which resulted in many of the newly recruited individuals departing the organization during the first year alone, and it didn't stop there. For the first few years, employee turnover rates remained high. We incurred substantial costs to identify, hire, develop, engage, and retain employees. This included additional related costs, such as overtime payments to replacement employees while suitable candidates were being recruited and onboarded. In general, millions of dollars are spent annually on recruitment in medium to large organizations, even more so in organizations plagued by high employee turnover.

We understood that the financial cost of high employee turnover wasn't the only loss we incurred. Employee disengagement negatively affects the overall customer experience, costing money and impacting the company's reputation.

Over the course of a decade, I dedicated my life to reducing employee attrition and employee turnover costs. Our journey also yielded a 26% increase in employee engagement, measured regularly through surveys. Favorable scores in areas such as internal communication, employee wellbeing, work–life balance, organizational development, and leadership perception soared to new heights.

The fruits of our labor did not go unnoticed. I was personally honored with numerous industry accolades, including "HR Person of the Year" from *Hotelier Middle East* magazine and "Manager of the Year," bestowed by my workplace. Our team and company also received several prestigious industry awards, such as "Best Employer" from Kincentric, "Best Employer Brand" from GCC Best Employer Brand Awards, "Best CSR Employee Engagement of the Year" and "Corporate Wellness Team of the Year" from Daman Corporate Health Awards, and "Best Employee Reward and Recognition Program" from the Brass Ring Human Resources Excellence IAAPA.

Education has always played a pivotal role in my journey to success. I hold a Bachelor of Communication with honors and an MBA, providing me with a solid foundation to understand business needs. Armed with this knowledge, I confidently partnered with and advised business units on how a great employee experience seamlessly translates into an exceptional customer experience and, in turn, drives outstanding business results. In 2019, I furthered my education, completing a Master of Science in Applied Positive Psychology. This additional expertise armed me with the tools to enhance employee engagement and happiness in various workplace settings.

My tenure at Aldar Properties, one of the largest real estate development, education, and investment companies in the UAE, allowed me to craft the blueprint, lay the foundations, and shape the culture and strategy for the employee experience. This journey involved collaborating with every facet of HR and engaging with employees and the leadership team.

I am committed to helping organizations create an exceptional employee experience through an innovative signature framework. I've witnessed firsthand the stark contrast between uninspiring workplaces and those that ignite passion and purpose. The results are both impressive and transformative. A highly engaged workforce reflects on and positively impacts the employee experience. This contributes to an increase in employee productivity, a reduction in the total cost of employee turnover, and an unforgettable guest experience that fosters unwavering customer loyalty.

As I embark on this journey with you, dear reader, I am filled with excitement and humility. I look forward to sharing this signature framework with you in the chapters that follow.

This book is a product of passion and dedication, with zero help from ChatGPT, born from over two decades of personal and professional experiences. It represents the culmination of hundreds and thousands of hours of academic and workplace research and practice, encapsulating the essence of my Master of Science in Applied Positive Psychology and drawing from a wealth of textbooks, books, journal articles, and white papers.

I've distilled these insights into a concise and engaging narrative, with a reference list at the end for your convenience.

May your experience reading this book be outstanding!

CHAPTER 2

VISION UNVEILED—
THE GRAND PERSPECTIVE

Sometimes, in our professional lives, we fail to see how every action and every decision is interconnected. The ripples of one choice can extend far into the future, shaping our experiences and those of our colleagues and customers. In this chapter, I unveil the big picture within workplaces, illustrating how every facet of work exerts a ripple effect on the experiences of all involved.

Beyond Employee Engagement is a journey for anyone seeking to make a profound difference in the world. Many of us spend almost an entire lifetime working, and our experiences at work deeply influence our lives and those around us. Workplaces can contribute positively to their employees, customers, and entire communities. They can do this through growing, training, and educating their workforce. They can motivate and reward exemplary behavior, which may in turn change how employees raise their children. They may also use effective, honest, transparent, and frequent communication, which creates meaningful connections and changes how they interact with those around them.

In this book's initial section, I will provide a high-level overview of the employee experience framework. The touchpoints in the framework will be broken down into detailed sections and chapters throughout this book. The last section will take you through some metrics of success that are crucial for building a robust business case for prioritizing the employee experience.

To be more specific and to set your expectations about the style of this book, in the chapters that follow, I share a blend of personal insights, research-based facts, and practical guidance on what can influence an employee's experience and, subsequently, a customer's experience. Together with you, I

will unravel the enigma of employee engagement and its influences, which are often hidden in plain sight. Recruiters may
think that all they are doing is selecting, interviewing, and hiring
candidates when they are actually influencing people's perception of the employer brand before they even join the organization. HR may think that all they need to do to onboard a
new employee is show them where the bathrooms and the coffee machine are; in reality, they are impacting and influencing
the very first minutes, hours, and days of the employee experience—and arguably the part most employees will remember
the most. The hiring manager is integral and potentially one of
the biggest influencers of the employee experience. Training,
development, growth, communication, problem-solving, and
engagement are all, to a certain degree, in the hands of the hiring manager when it comes to the long-term employee journey
and, contrary to popular belief, not in the hands of programs
that are championed by HR.

In the last decade, wellbeing has become a non-negotiable
part of many corporate cultures. We'll explore the various dimensions of wellbeing, delving beyond physical and mental health
to understand how a holistic approach transforms the employee
journey and, consequently, the customer experience.

Our exploration extends to the realm of the customer experience. We'll examine the evolving landscape of the experience
economy and emphasize that businesses must think beyond offering a mere service. Customers often seek unforgettable experiences; they want an emotional event they can relish and discuss
with their loved ones. Beyond the experience, they want a transformation that will touch them emotionally and mentally, a service
they will want to use repeatedly, and a service they will tell their

friends about. The customer experience chapter talks about how businesses can create experiences and how to stage them imaginatively, and about creating economic value for customers. The key to delivering these experiences lies in the employees. However, for them to be emotionally invested, their own journey at work must be inspiring and fulfilling.

Subsequent chapters will define the touchpoints along an employee's journey, from initial contact to retirement and beyond. These major touchpoints along the road begin as early as the first time you hear about a company. You could hear the name of a company in a conversation with your neighbor whose son was poorly treated by his manager and fired unjustly, or it could be because the cashier in your local supermarket has been so well-trained and mentored that she is now the store manager. Employer branding, or the company's reputation as an employer, plays a significant role in the beginning stage of the employee experience. This is followed by factors such as recruitment and how interviews are conducted, the involvement of your future manager, and how the team makes you feel during your first month at work. The employee experience is influenced by factors such as the physical and technological environment, but mainly by the organization's culture.

Our journey takes us on a cultural tour, where I provide ample food for thought that will help you understand the foundations of company culture and how to build it. I go on to discuss who is responsible for spreading it, delineating the role of leaders and culture champions. Toxic cultures have far-reaching consequences, affecting not only the workplace but also homes, neighborhoods, and entire communities. That is why colleagues at all levels, including senior leaders and HR teams, must constantly strive to create and transform workplaces into positive and inspirational experiences where people are encouraged to do their best and be the best version of themselves.

As you read on, we will delve into the crucial task of attracting suitable candidates who resonate with a company's vision and mission. Talented and committed individuals who are motivated to go above and beyond, and who receive the necessary recognition and growth opportunities, will undoubtedly create an outstanding customer experience. But, for that to happen, potential candidates must feel that initial sense of connection to the company. This could be because they have similar core values or because people feel a calling to a particular profession and the industry itself is a big motivator for them, but that's not enough. We'll explore the importance of alignment in the interviewing and hiring process and how a welcoming, engaging, informative, and tailor-made onboarding experience sets the stage for employee success.

At the heart of the employee experience, I emphasize creating high-performing cultures that focus on engagement and empowerment through growth, learning, development, and wellbeing programs. There is a dedicated section on how workplaces can use positive psychology and well-executed internal communication strategies to engage individuals and teams and help them feel a deep sense of meaning and belonging.

The journey of employee engagement, learning, and development is ongoing and woven into the fabric of the employee experience. It spans beyond singular touchpoints such as hiring, onboarding, or exiting and is a continuous path toward growth and excellence. With the help of empowering growth policies, well-thought-out engagement strategies, and company-wide rewards and recognition programs, individuals can reach their full potential and establish meaningful connections. These kinds of experiences can be transformative for employees, customers, and the wider community.

The book's last section centers around an employee's exit, be it voluntary or involuntary. Great workplaces prioritize professionalism, transparency, and empathy equally for all individuals, whether they are entering or leaving the company. Treating someone who has been terminated with dignity and respect shows a level of maturity that all companies should aspire to reach. Employee advocacy is gaining recognition as a significant and influential force in the workplace. Let's remember that a person leaving the organization is someone who can also return. If this individual is a talented employee who has contributed to a positive and supportive work environment, then companies should want them to want to return one day and should be doing something about it.

Lastly, the discussion on metrics provides a comprehensive understanding of how various measurements and research methodologies can illustrate the impact of employer branding, engagement, internal communication, wellbeing, rewards, recognition, and development strategies on the entire employee experience.

This complete blueprint will help you understand how to create legendary workplace cultures that lead to outstanding employee experiences and phenomenal customer experiences. Imagine the transformation in profitability when employee engagement elevates customer satisfaction, reduces attrition rates, and amplifies employee pride.

Our actions at work can profoundly impact those around us—from our colleagues to our customers to our communities.

Let's embark on a journey through the pages of this book, where we can work together to make a difference and create a better world through the everyday actions we take in our workplaces. Understanding this grand perspective will help us achieve our goal. Together, we can inspire positive change and leave a lasting impact on the world.

CHAPTER 3

THE CUSTOMER EXPERIENCE IN THE EXPERIENCE ECONOMY

*"We see our customers as invited guests to a party,
and we are the hosts. It is our job every day to make
every important aspect of the customer
experience a little bit better."*

— JEFF BEZOS

Every 'customer-obsessed' Amazon employee lives and breathes these thoughts. But why? To what end?

It's all about the customer. I invite you to join me in looking at the evolution of the customer experience and to better understand the significance of a truly memorable and transformational customer experience. By the end of this chapter, your knowledge of how a customer experience is designed, shaped, and individualized will influence your view on how you do business. In this chapter, we will review several models for an outstanding experience and look at how these can be adopted in the workplace.

For companies in any industry to build on their competitive advantage, they must offer experiences. Goods and services are no longer enough. Creating positive, memorable experiences that engage customers personally is a sure way to stand out. Walt Disney, one of the most iconic figures synonymous with the customer experience, famously said, "Whatever you do, do it well. Do it so well that when people see you do it, they'll want to come back and see you do it again, and they will want to bring others and show them how well you do what you do." What do you think this means? How is it relevant to you in the context of your work? Whatever your answer is, one of the reasons you're reading this book is that you want to become even better at what you currently do and how you do it. Come with me on a learning journey, on an exploration toward a transformational customer experience created just for you! Let's go!

MY 40TH BIRTHDAY CELEBRATION

The BIG 40! I wanted it to be extraordinary, experiential, and memorable. It would be another ten years before I entered a new decade, so this was a big deal for me!

I love the cinema. I grew up with movies. I studied cinema theory as part of my bachelor's degree, and I could not think of a better way to commemorate my birthday than immersing myself and my loved ones in this passion. So, we decided to celebrate at the Paramount Hotel in Dubai. The minute you enter the hotel, you are transported into the world of cinema, from the uniquely themed uniforms of the bell-services team to the receptionists—known not as receptionists but as front-stage agents—all led by the front-stage producer! I felt like the star of my own movie, and everyone around me was a supporting actor. The movie-themed check-in desks and cladded elevators set high expectations for our personalized suite. Yes, we stayed in a suite. We were upgraded, and because it was my special day, we were given an offer we could not refuse! The Godfather Suite was everything you can imagine and more: memorabilia, food amenities, technology, art, and furniture (they even had a barber's chair and fancy mirrors in the walk-in closet area). It was magical and immersive. We could rent our own private cinema for forty-five guests and watch any of our favorite Paramount specials. The dinner celebration was held at an interactive speakeasy-themed restaurant that staged a murder mystery dinner set in the 1920s. Characters, singers, and actors in full costume ensured that we all participated in solving the crime and prevented another one from happening. It was a sensational show from start to end and an experience I do not plan to forget. I subsequently visited again several times so other friends could experience it, too.

As I propose how you, too, can set your stage for success, I think about all the ways this birthday celebration perfectly exemplified the principles I will outline. Let's get started, and you will see what I mean!

STEP INTO THE WORLD OF THE EXPERIENCE ECONOMY

The term 'experience economy' was coined a little over two decades ago by Pine and Gilmore—internationally acclaimed authors, speakers, and management advisors to Fortune 500 companies. It refers to the act of being customer-*centric* rather than just customer-*focused*. Switching a business's mindset from reactively selling to proactively serving and being mindful of crafting emotionally authentic customer relationships are at the helm of the experience economy. People undeniably want better experiences, and successfully competitive companies are in the business of providing just that. Extraordinary experiences are inherently personal and are primarily formed in the hearts and minds of people who have been captivated on emotional, physical, intellectual, and spiritual levels. Everyone's experience is different because it is derived from an individual's perception of the provided service. However, employing engaged and caring employees is not the only factor in creating such experiences; there is much more to it, as you will see.

Experiences are a significant component of industries such as travel, tourism, hospitality, food and beverage ('eatertainment'), malls ('shoppertainment'), amusement parks, theatres, retail ... the list goes on. But what about gas stations? What about hospitals? Aren't hospitals hotels for the ill? And shouldn't they aim to give their guests the same authentic and genuine experience as hotels and resorts? Even academic institutions such as museums consider the concept of 'edutainment' as a learning modality! This doesn't refer to simply having fun, spending money, etc. Instead, it's really about creating a richer, more personal and memorable experience for the customer. Fantastic experiences are not an accident; they occur by design. At the helm of such experiences is a well-thought-out strategy, but flawless execution is equally important. As such, the people in charge of providing those great experiences have a noteworthy role to play.

WHAT YOU NEED TO KNOW ABOUT DESIGNING EXPERIENCES

Pine and Gilmore's *Four Realms of an Experience* (Figure 1) offers a unique perspective on the different types of experiences. Based on their location along two dimensions, experiences can be categorized into four types. The first dimension is customer 'participation,' which ranges from passive (watching the opera) to active (participating in an escape room). The second dimension is 'connection,' which determines whether an experience is absorbing or immersive. Pine and Gilmore suggest that for an experience to be truly satisfying, it should encompass all four realms, represented by the round area where the two dimensions meet.

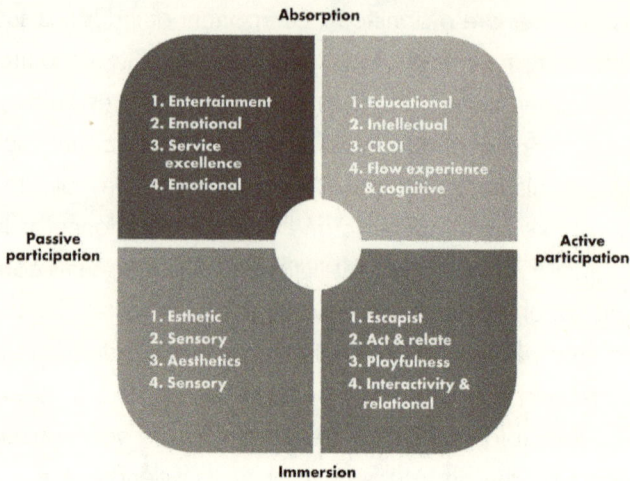

FIGURE 1. THE FOUR REALMS OF AN EXPERIENCE

When designing a memorable, immersive experience, Pine and Gilmore suggest that you adhere to five fundamental design principles. These design principles can be utilized for any kind of experience or industry.

Think about how you can creatively apply these principles to design an excellent internal and external customer experience at your workplace.

- **Theming the experience.** The theme and design elements must tell a unified story. This does not need to be publicly articulated, such as, for example, theming a toy store with a Barbie and Ken theme.
- **Harmonizing impressions with positive cues.** Realistic and authentic themes, narratives, decorations, language used with customers, and behavior of employees are all essential. This can even be noticed from how you are greeted.

- **Eliminating negative cues.** Oversupplying positive cues never makes up for the bad ones. Over-servicing is not a way to improve the experience—for example, waiters coming to interrupt your meal by asking if you are enjoying your food multiple times or call-center agents taking too long because of their lengthy, obviously scripted robotic pleasantries.
- **Selling memorabilia.** People buy memorabilia if they have enjoyed the experience and want to be reminded of its uniqueness, such as at the end of a Cirque du Soleil performance or after a Hans Zimmer concert.
- **Engaging all five senses.** As much as possible, think of the visual, audio, smell, taste, and touch when creating an experience journey.

Immersing all five senses cannot be understated, regardless of the type of customer experience being designed. I had the opportunity to visit a unique art installation that showcased Van Gogh's paintings in a digital and immersive format. The experience was truly mesmerizing, with stunning visuals and accompanying sound effects. Another example of sensory engagement is IKEA's famous Swedish meatballs, which add homey smells and tastes to the shopping experience, thus influencing customers to purchase furniture. The Dubai Expo 2020 was a remarkable project that successfully engaged all five senses of over twenty-four million visitors during its six-month run. It was truly a wondrous and intricate endeavor.

Simply offering customized commodities, goods, and services is no longer enough for an experience-based provider to stand out. The experiences they provide must also be tailored to their clientele. The focus should be on creating personalized, engaging, authentic, and meaningful experiences for participants, including their interactions with other customers and employees. Employees can enhance these experiences and make them truly special.

Now that we've covered the fundamentals of designing an intentional experiential customer journey, let's explore how to elevate the experience to exceptional levels.

Pine and Gilmore have co-authored several textbooks and multiple journal articles on this topic. They are also cofounders of Strategic Horizons LLP, a thinking studio dedicated to helping companies design new ways of adding value to their offerings. They pinpoint five value-creating opportunities as key drivers of success in the experience economy:

1. **Customizing goods.** More offerings should be mass-*customized* instead of mass-*produced* (i.e., made to fit the individual needs of customers and produced according to what they want, when they want it)—for example, having your name engraved on a perfume bottle.
2. **Enhancing services.** Put yourself in the customer's shoes and determine how to enhance, innovate, speed up, and create a better way of doing business with them. It's not only about the tasks employees do, but also everything they do *not* do. Consider here the importance of serving free healthy drinks and providing fruit in the lobby of a hospital.
3. **Charging for experiences.** A considerable source for continuous improvement is asking yourself what you would do differently if you were to charge for it. This question challenges business owners to be innovative and create extra revenue by charging for additional experiences that people will happily pay for—for example, providing a personal concierge service at the airport.

4. **Fusing digital technology with reality.** Businesses must leverage digital technology and integrate it into everyday life to avoid losing customer attention—for example, a pop-up chatbot during an online shopping experience that uses AI to show you what an outfit can look like on you.

5. **Transformative experiences.** The experience economy is evolving into the transformative economy, which offers a journey that leads to positive memories, changes, and lasting benefits. In this type of economy, the customer is the actual product, as seen when paying for a personal trainer at the gym. These transformative journeys leave a lasting impression on the hearts and minds of the experiencers. If experiences are not transformational, they may become less enjoyable with repetition. This can, however, be avoided by customization.

Let's now look at a different model that talks about the customer experience and how this can be combined with the Pine and Gilmore model.

THE EXPERIENCE PYRAMID MODEL

In 2009, Sanna Tarssanen, a customer experience professional from Finland, created the *Experience Pyramid Model* (Figure 2) for creating outstanding, meaningful guest experiences. Tarssanen emphasized the importance of considering all the elements and levels of a customer experience. In Tarssanen's model, guests' experiences are influenced by the factors shown on the horizontal axis. It is important to include all these elements in their journey to create lasting memories. The vertical axis represents the levels of experience that define the guests' journeys.

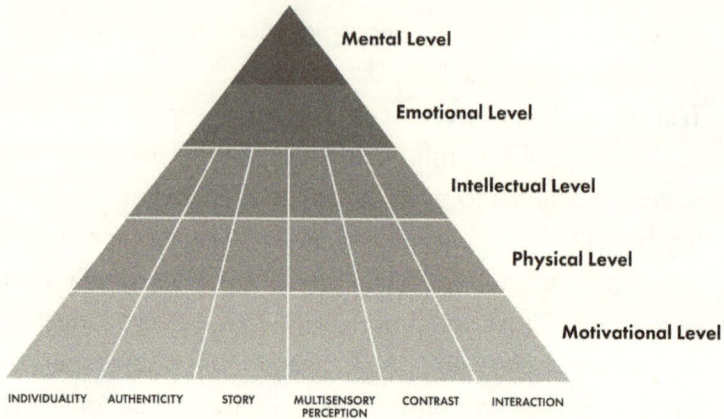

FIGURE 2. TARSSANEN'S EXPERIENCE PYRAMID MODEL

The motivational level begins by captivating participants and using innovative marketing techniques to ignite their curiosity and drive. The participants in the experience should be engrossed in the theme and activity, to the point where their sense of reality is altered (safely). At the physical level, it is of the utmost importance to create an immersive, safe environment that caters to participants' physical and physiological needs before tapping into the intellectual, emotional, and mental levels of the model.

The intellectual level can be activated by incorporating educational elements that broaden horizons and encourage personal growth. Here, participants are looking for a meaningful experience. This approach may vary depending on the industry, but the impact on the participants should undoubtedly be transformative.

The emotional and mental levels of the experience pyramid are separated from the other levels because they are subjective for each guest and are not necessarily controlled by the designer. Businesses that create personalized products, services, and experiences that evoke positive emotions tend to have greater customer loyalty. From a mental perspective, a well-designed experience should elicit a meaningful and lasting transformation, including a change in behavior or way of thinking, rethinking one's values, discovering a strength, or acquiring a hobby.

The community management provider who oversees my residential community is an excellent example of an employee who works constantly to incorporate the different elements of the experience pyramid into their service. Typically, community management companies take care of the safety and security of residents, landscaping, and housekeeping of the roads and parks. In my case, the community management provider goes a step further to build connections and foster a sense of community through various activities, such as a monthly newsletter with updates on improvements, community events, parties, and sports days. Additionally, they motivate residents to care for the environment by organizing activities such as tree-planting days, desert clean-ups, and educational activities centered around bees, their hives, and honey-making. The aim is to appeal to the residents on an intellectual level to promote camaraderie and engagement, while also encouraging philanthropic efforts and changes in behavior, ways of thinking, and eventually transformation.

IS THAT ALL?

I find Pine and Gilmore's perspective on the evolution of the customer-experience journey fascinating. According to them, customizing a 'good' turns it into a service, customizing a service can turn it into an experience, and customizing an experience can result in a transformation. In today's competitive market, companies that can provide personalized services to their customers, thereby positively impacting their lives, will stand out and win their time, attention, money, and loyalty.

To elevate the customer experience at your workplace, take a moment to reflect on the Four Realms of an Experience (Figure 1) and how the principles of exceptional customer experience design can be applied internally and externally. Incorporating the Experience Pyramid Model into your overall guest experience strategy will further facilitate unforgettable customer experiences.

THAT'S ALL, FOLKS!

Throughout this chapter, we looked at the importance of theming an experience and simultaneously harmonizing impressions with positive cues whilst eliminating negative ones. The notion of engaging all five senses while designing an excellent experience and selling memorabilia was also discussed. To elevate experiences further, businesses must look at how to customize their goods, enhance their products, and determine what they would do better if they were to charge for an experience they currently provide for free (or don't offer at all). Fusing digital technology with reality to retain customers' attention and eventually offer transformative experiences was explored. Lastly, the Experience Pyramid Model was presented to reinforce and solidify considerations to produce a remarkable and significant customer experience. Is that everything? Is it truly that straightforward?

After gaining the knowledge to create an exceptional guest experience, it's crucial to recognize the employee role. Many people fail to understand the link between the designed experience and the human beings (usually) delivering it. Even if you have an impressively designed guest experience, it's useless if the people delivering it aren't emotionally connected to your company. Therefore, it's imperative to understand the influence of a remarkable employee experience in creating an outstanding guest experience. Employees at the helm of providing outstanding and transformational customer experiences must understand the importance of their role and be fully empowered to deliver those experiences. How can companies help with that?

The first step towards creating an extraordinary customer experience is the exclusive, personalized, and continuous focus on the employee experience! When striving to add value to the guest experience, we must consider the involvement and experience of the employees themselves. They bring the customer experience strategy to life, infusing it with their unique touch, which can make all the difference. By ensuring that employees have had a firsthand experience of what it means to deliver an outstanding customer experience, we can promote more excellent business continuity and future success. When we go above and beyond in treating employees well and making their employee experience outstanding, they will, in turn, extend that same positive energy to customers. Not every company embraces the link between the employee experience (eX) and the customer experience (cX). This connection is key, as it represents a genuine and meaningful relationship between individuals that can profoundly impact operations.

Sir Richard Branson famously said, "Take care of your employees, and they will take care of your business. It's as simple as that.

Healthy, engaged employees are your top competitive advantage." What does this mean to you as a leader? How do you apply it at your workplace, and can you do better?

How do you envisage your employee experience? Personal, memorable, engaging ... ? Whatever your vision is, reading on will help you understand precisely how you can make it come to life (or improve what you currently offer).

CHALLENGE ACCEPTED: PUTTING *THE EMPLOYEE EXPERIENCE* INTO ACTION

Here are some recommended activities. I will be sharing selected tasks at the end of each chapter. Remember, small but impactful changes can significantly influence the overall employee experience. Start with these challenges and experiment to find what works best for your unique company culture.

1. Measure and Motivate

Task: Do some preliminary research to understand your employees' perspectives on their journey with your company.

Challenge: Analyze the data you collect to identify areas for improvement. Focus on gathering both quantitative and qualitative data to get a nuanced understanding of employee sentiment. After reading Chapter 14 on Metrics, do this exercise again and see how your newly acquired knowledge will help.

Activity: Share the results with your wider team and decision-makers and develop an action plan to address the key areas of concern. Also, share the plan and progress with employees to foster trust and engagement.

2. Champion & Connect

Task: Identify and empower 'experience champions' across departments who are passionate about overall employee wellbeing.

Challenge: Encourage these champions to organize a calendar of social events or teambuilding activities to build connections and boost morale.

Activity: Create a recognition program for outstanding champions and showcase their initiatives to inspire others to get involved.

CHAPTER 4

THE EMPLOYEE EXPERIENCE JOURNEY

*"Customers will never love a company
until the employees love it first."*

—SIMON SINEK

You have the power to make this happen as a leader. This chapter will give you meaningful insight and guidance on building trust and inspiring your employees to love their company with a holistic employee experience strategy. This will help them deliver customized guest experiences that will subsequently increase your customers' net promoter scores and their loyalty.

This chapter will also discuss the employee experience (eX) and how to create a positive, memorable one. It will define the employee experience and the various touchpoints of the employee journey and look at ways organizations can influence moments that matter for employees and their loved ones through design thinking, employee feedback, compassion, empathy, and kindness. This is important because the overall employee experience has so much influence over employee engagement, employee retention, the cost of employee turnover, productivity, performance, development, absenteeism, employee and employer branding, business revenue and profit, innovation, customer and investor experiences and ultimately the experiences of communities and societies. Research shows that employees with positive experiences at work will go above and beyond to deliver exceptional customer experiences. Their experiences will affect their feelings about their job's purpose, culture, and employee brand. They will also influence their decision to return to previous employers and their willingness to recommend their organization to other potential candidates.

I have packed this chapter with vital, well-designed research findings and priceless advice from companies such as Gallup, as well as individual scholars such as author and speaker Jacob Morgan—but that's not all. Throughout this chapter, I continue to impart expertise amassed over twenty years of my professional career through studying, trial and error, and genuinely connecting with human beings. Are you ready? Buckle up, and let the journey begin!

WHAT IS THE EMPLOYEE EXPERIENCE?

The eX is the journey that employees have at their workplace. It is a journey that the employee and the employer take together. It is a roadmap that traces the experience of an employee from hiring to retirement and beyond. Along the road, between these touch-points, we can see significant moments that matter in a person's life. Milestones.

Constructs such as workplace flexibility, wellbeing, organizational culture, a sense of purpose and belonging—all these and much more constitute the employee experience. Since the onset of the global COVID-19 pandemic in 2020, how we work has undeniably changed and complicated certain aspects of the employee journey more than others, drastically in some industries and moderately in others. Managing the current workforce has become exponentially more complex, and the pandemic is responsible for much of this.

When I began working in this field in 2008, employee engagement—the older relative of employee experience—had been around since the early 1990s. Even earlier, organizations focused on employee satisfaction (employee contentment). However, over the decades, and with people's changing priorities, this conversation has evolved from employee satisfaction to employee engagement to the overall employee experience. This is more than just a change in phraseology, and those who truly understand it will be able to reap the business benefits and craft a strategic competitive advantage.

As defined by Gallup, the employee experience constitutes the sum of all interactions an employee has with their employer from pre-recruitment to post-exit. According to subject-matter expert and bestselling author Jacob Morgan, *the employee experience* can be summed up as the totality of the cultural, physical, and technological environment an employee works in. With my professional experience and the help of customer-experience creator experts such as Pine and Gilmore (discussed in the previous chapter), I will unpack these theories and demystify the notion of the employee experience and how you can create an awesome journey for your workplace!

WHY SHOULD I SPEND TIME AND MONEY ON IT?

Your employee branding (the way employees feel about their workplace) and your employer branding (the way external potential candidates think about your workplace) impact your company's reputation, which in turn can attract or deter high-performing talent. An employee who has left the company and had a positive employee experience will continue to be your brand ambassador long after they have left. Those experiencing a fantastic workplace are likelier to stay, develop, and grow. This affects not only them but also their families and, oftentimes, the communities in which they live. Furthermore, the employee experience directly influences customer experience and profitability.

These are all fantastic reasons to invest in a great employee experience that emotionally touches and engages all employees. According to the 2023 State of the Global Workplace Report by Gallup, low engagement can have a significant impact, costing $8.8 trillion or the equivalent of 9% of global GDP. This highlights the importance of ensuring individuals are motivated and engaged in their work, as it contributes greatly to the success of humanity.

Let's also factor in the cost of employee turnover. According to renowned turnover expert, author, and keynote speaker Richard Finnegan, employee turnover costs an enormous sum of money that companies spend annually to hire new employees and replace the ones who have left. My colleagues and I diligently studied Finnegan's work and calculated that, on average, one colleague in a non-managerial role leaving our workplace was costing between $4,000 and $6,000! The cost of one manager or senior leader leaving the company was, on average, $9,600–$11,600. Of course, these figures depend on remuneration, benefits, hiring costs, and other factors that will vary from industry to industry and from country to country.

I invite you to do the math and calculate how much your company spends annually on new hires. If you want to find that number even faster, Finnegan offers his readers a cost-of-turnover calculator. That should convince you and all the senior leaders that you should focus your attention on creating a fantastic eX so colleagues are engaged and do not wish to leave. Inspired employees will create a fantastic cX.

DEVELOPING AN EMPLOYEE EXPERIENCE STRATEGY

According to Gallup, when developing a compelling and authentic eX, one should consider several factors:

- aligning the eX to reflect the company's purpose, employer brand culture, and organizational identity
- focusing on the stages of the employee lifecycle
- keeping the core needs of employees in mind:
  - the relationship of a colleague with their manager
  - the clarity of their role
  - the value they add to the organization
  - the physical workspace
  - their overall engagement and wellbeing
  - opportunities for personal development and growth.

A good starting point is identifying the crucial stages of the employee lifecycle and the different touchpoints employees will encounter. This can be used as a roadmap or framework. For companies who may already have a strategy and are looking to improve it, the best way forward will be design thinking and utilizing the voices of your entire team to help with continuous improvement.

The stages of the employee lifecycle are:

1. attracting potential talented candidates
2. hiring selected superstars
3. onboarding and welcoming them to the organization
4. engaging them with their job, their colleagues, and their workplace (ongoing)

5. performance enhancement—helping them to be successful (ongoing)
6. developing their careers and potentially cross-boarding to a different entity or sister company (ongoing)
7. departing them from the organization (ideally with an excellent experience)
8. potentially reboarding.

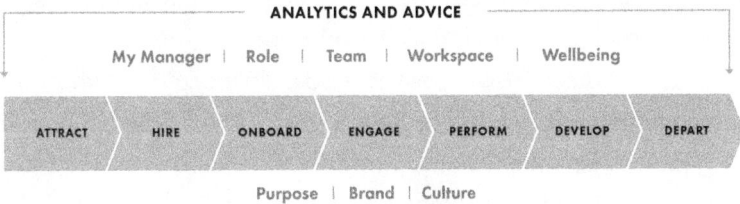

ANALYTICS AND ADVICE

My Manager | Role | Team | Workspace | Wellbeing

ATTRACT | HIRE | ONBOARD | ENGAGE | PERFORM | DEVELOP | DEPART

Purpose | Brand | Culture

GALLUP

FIGURE 3. OVERVIEW OF THE EMPLOYEE EXPERIENCE JOURNEY, AS PRESENTED BY GALLUP

THE PEOPLE-CENTRIC EXPERIENCE

Each stage of the employee lifecycle must be intentionally activated according to your company culture to demonstrate your vision of an excellent employee experience. The eX strategy must be interwoven throughout these critical stages to create a meaningful journey for every colleague at every level, considering their interactions with their peers and leaders. It is best to involve colleagues from various departments and consider other demographics such as age, gender, ethnicity, nationality, company tenure, level, education, and marital status. People support what they create; they feel invested in it. Employees should participate in the ongoing creation of experiences for themselves and their

BEYOND EMPLOYEE ENGAGEMENT

colleagues. Leaders should design and implement systems for continuous positive experience development amongst everyone in the company. Allow your employees to help build a great ongoing employee experience for themselves and others by taking into consideration their opinions and getting their buy-in.

Let's keep in mind that permanent full-time employees are not the only ones that are affected by an eX. What about hourly employees, suppliers, contractors, volunteers, and others? How are they treated? What is their experience?

Can you visualize the path of a potential candidate who joins the company and works for three years? How do you envisage their journey from the first time they hear about you to the last interaction as they depart? What about a year after that? What are they saying to their friends about you? Would they come back and work with you or your company?

These stages will be discussed in the chapters that follow, and I will detail what organizations can do along each stage of the cycle to make the eX positively memorable.

WHAT FACTORS INFLUENCE THE EMPLOYEE EXPERIENCE?

In one of his bestselling books, *The Employee Experience Advantage*, Jacob Morgan refers to the concept of employee engagement as a short-term adrenalin injection. Instead of focusing on employee engagement, which is what companies worldwide have been doing, he encourages organizations to concentrate on the long-term (re)design of an organization, which is ongoing and puts employees first. This is the employee experience. The eX is shaped and influenced by both employees and the organization. As such, organizations create our work environment, but the employees play a significant role in shaping the overall experience.

Morgan talks about the environment that must be created for employees to have a great experience at work. He breaks it down into three aspects that constitute every single employee experience at every organization worldwide: physical environment, technological environment, and cultural environment.

The physical and technological environments together account for 60% of the employee experience, whilst the cultural environment contributes 40% of the employee experience.

THE PHYSICAL ENVIRONMENT

The physical workspace is somewhere people should *want* to be and not *need* to be. It accounts for 30% of the eX.

As such, the physical environment is what one can see, touch, taste, hear, and smell. This includes everything from the walking-in experience to the art on the walls, the office/desk space, and even the demographics of the people you work with. It includes all the tangible benefits, such as the employee restaurant, gym, relaxation/games areas, smoking area, meeting rooms and spaces, coffee shops, and more. Workplace flexibility, autonomy, and access to multiple workspaces affect this environment. Morgan advises that an excellent physical environment should be COOL:

C = **Choose** to bring friends or visitors to a space we are proud of

O = Organizational values are reflected
O = Offers flexibility in terms of hours and space (hybrid, remote, and onsite work)
L = Leverages multiple workspace options with multiple office space types for collaboration and quiet work.

I have worked in open-space environments where it was so noisy and distracting that I always used headphones. This was not conducive to welcoming customers; it was also not very comfortable. Conversely, I have worked in an environment where the art on the wall was fun, inspiring, and gave me a sense of pride, and I gladly invited my mother to visit from time to time.

I invite you to picture the places you have worked or currently work and identify how they make you feel. Are you willing to bring your friends and relatives to experience the environment, or would you be ashamed?

THE TECHNOLOGICAL ENVIRONMENT

This environment refers to the tools employees use to get work done. While technology is just one factor contributing to an employee's overall experience, it is significant. Technology shapes an organization's culture and influences how employees interact with the physical workspace. It comprises 30% of the eX.

Companies that want a competitive advantage, higher revenue, and better customer and employee loyalty must focus on offering ACE technologies to their colleagues. What is ACE technology?

A = Available to everyone in the company who requires it for work

C = Consumer-grade technology, meaning the quality is so good that you can sell it to customers; ideally, it is tailored to a person's job role

E = Employee needs + business requirements are met 100%.

Colleagues use technology to connect to the organization before they are even hired, which saves them time once they start work. Think about the online job application experience, the hiring and onboarding process, the remote or hybrid working technology, the intranet, the suite of HR systems, and all the other software needed for colleagues to create an excellent guest experience. Picture a scenario where all of these are state-of-the-art, easy to use, free, and available to everyone. Now, imagine a scenario where they desperately need updating, improving, or even changing! People want quick and easy access to their tools—it's as simple as that. It's not only about the tools they utilize for their personal needs, such as an onboarding platform or a time and attendance system. It's also about the software they use daily to serve customers, such as a finance platform to collect payment. As a company, how effectively are you taking advantage of technology that saves people time?

In a former workplace, the leadership team changed the HR system. This system was used by the HR team and the other departments' administrators for time and attendance, payroll and overtime calculation, holiday-leave calculation and application, new applicant tracking, and all the other HR-related functions. For years we'd used a great HR system, which was replaced with a second-grade one to save costs. However, the new system was so terrible that it took people much longer to finish their work! This created aggravation and errors, and it didn't save the company money. Instead, it was the reason for cultural entropy, disengagement, disgruntlement, resignations, and an overall horrid employee experience. We even had to hire more employees just to handle the extra work created by the system! It was a crucial mistake that saw long-lasting repercussions.

An excellent example of technology use is what Microsoft did. They created an interactive technology solution to guide employees through their first 90 days and provide ongoing development afterward. Microsoft noticed that regular, one-on-one meetings between employees and managers significantly impacted employee engagement. They decided to develop the Responsive Career Guide, a workplace technology that guides employees during their first 90 days. Using communications, collaboration, and social capabilities to connect people, information, and resources, the technology reduced onboarding time and training costs while improving employee retention and the eX.

Another great example is Unily's Employee Journeys. This feature allows consumers to build their intranets around the employee experience. On their very first day, they have a pop-up welcoming them to the intranet platform and pointing them in the direction of all the tools they need, such as the colleague handbook and office guidelines. Then, at various, pre-defined stages along their employee journey (e.g., after three months), they might be directed to a 'How are we doing?' form, asking them for their feedback on their journey so far. Before a transfer to another position, potentially in a different country, they may automatically be asked to complete a cultural competency exercise to ensure they are familiar with the location they are moving to. Technology, which was once one-dimensional, is now key to intelligently enhancing the employee experience with very little manual intervention.

With the COVID-19 pandemic, it has become even more apparent that employees require greater flexibility in terms of workspace, hours, and travel. This should be considered when planning ACE technologies for the workforce.

THE CULTURAL ENVIRONMENT

The cultural environment has the most considerable influence on the eX, accounting for 40%. Culture is the vibe you get when you come to work. This includes the language and tone used; the behavior and attitude of senior leaders with colleagues and vice versa; the organizational values, mission, and vision; and the employer value proposition. It is the mood and the tone the workplace sets. It is also how leaders interact with one another and whether they help instill a sense of purpose, meaning, and belonging among the employees.

Culture is the living personality of the organization. It is the air you breathe in an organization; it is everywhere, and everyone is impacted by it. The right culture energizes, empowers, and motivates employees; the wrong culture drains, suffocates, and discourages people. Organizations must be adaptable to their teams' changing needs. Organizations that listen to their employees and allow them to be authentic and show their vulnerability without fear of negative repercussions are the ones for which employees will go above and beyond to give back to the organization.

The physical spaces and technology could be amazing, but if the culture is toxic, the company is in grave danger of high turnover and low customer loyalty. I know this from personal experience, and I aim to spread my knowledge to help workplaces create a great culture where people are happy, thriving, and given an incredible experience.

The prerequisites for a great cultural environment that can be **CELEBRATED**, as proposed by Morgan, include:

C = Company is viewed positively and has an excellent employer and employee brand perception

E = Everyone feels valued and celebrated

L = Legitimate sense of purpose for all

E = Employees feel like they're part of a team; they belong

B = Believes in a diverse, inclusive, equal, and equitable environment

R = Referrals come from employees because they love their workplace so much that they refer others

A = Ability to learn new things and advance in their careers

T = Treats employees fairly and honestly, and there is transparent treatment for everyone

E = Executives and managers are coaches and mentors

D = Dedicated to, actively cares about, and focuses on employees' health and wellbeing.

CREATING MOMENTS THAT MATTER

When building the eX, it is paramount to consider the various stages of the employee lifecycle and the technological, physical, and cultural environments we all help create. Recognizing how employees' experiences are intentionally set up and staged is significant.

Essential moments are found at all stages of the employee lifecycle. These can include your first day at work during orientation, your first official welcome to the team, your first salary, your first recognition for doing something outstanding, and your first promotion or performance appraisal. It could be your birthday, work anniversary, wedding, or first file notation, the death of a loved one, or an official warning for something wrong. The list goes on.

Organizations must plan their eX strategies around the moments that matter to people. For instance, what are the top ten moments that matter during hiring and onboarding? What about the moments that matter during the growth cycle? How does your organization announce and celebrate promotions?

Start by assessing all your employee processes and procedures, and remember that this is not limited to HR policies but also includes those of the IT and finance departments and any other department that employees work with directly. Break it down further: Every team and every manager should be doing this, too. There must be countless employee processes and moments that HR professionals are not privy to. It could be the process between a hotel's front office and housekeeping, or the process between the sales team and the ticketing counters in an entertainment venue. Where can you save time? Where are you wasting people's time? Evaluate this and free up time so your employees can provide a more efficient service for guests.

Next, involve various personas to help them feel connected while building their own future experiences.

I interviewed Jason Cochran, an influential psychologist and growth culture expert, for this book. He proposes that a positive eX is impacted by the four principles of connection:

1. People are looking to **connect with themselves better**; they want to understand themselves. Organizations that help employees understand their own personal values, the beliefs they stand for, their strengths, their unique skill sets, and their talents are ahead of those who do not connect on a deep level with their employees.
2. People are looking to **connect with others**; organizations that help people connect in profound, authentic ways with others through engagement activities or coaching skills such as kindness, empathy, compassion, emotional intelligence, effective communication, and humility will ultimately help them feel connected to the organization.
3. People want to **connect to their roles**; they want to feel that their tasks and responsibilities are mission-critical to the organization. A great onboarding experience and subsequent leadership interaction will do just that.
4. People want to **connect to the organization**; they want to feel their contribution matters in the overall big picture. People must feel that they are part of the culture and must be invited to participate in it. This way, they will have an overall positive effect on their own employee experience and everyone else's.

The previous chapter looked at the experience economy and how business owners can shape and stage their customer experience. The authors that coined the phrase "experience economy," Pine and Gilmore, further identified five core principles and a framework they fit within when applied to the customer and the employee experience.

Experiences should be:

1. **Robust**. Experiences consider all aspects of the employees' day, such as the digital, cultural, physical, educational, escapist, aesthetic, and entertainment aspects.
2. **Cohesive**. Experiences fit all the elements discussed throughout this chapter into the organization's theme and make it cohesive from front to back.
3. **Personal**. Experiences should be customized to individuals or demographics by customizing the elements that go into each touchpoint along the employee experience journey.
4. **Transformative**. Experiences that are transformative help employees achieve aspirations and make personal and professional changes. This is often achieved with the help of the learning and development and talent management departments.
5. **Dynamic.** Experiences are dramatic, engaging, memorable, and evoke emotion. These can be the orientation program, the annual party, or even a career development fair!

Pine discusses the 5Es, adapted from a framework by Deloitte business Doblin, to create a dramatic structure:

1. Enticing (How alluring is it?)
2. Entering (What are their first impressions?)
3. Engaging (Were they immersed?)
4. Exiting (What happens at the end?)
5. Extending (How do you encourage repeat visits?).

Leaders can use these five Es to design the entire lifespan of employment. This will allow for a well-structured and holistic strategy.

MY SIGNATURE EX METHOD

Now that you have a tangible understanding of the physical, technological, and cultural environments and key moments that matter to employees, we can create an inspiring roadmap by focusing on the seven essential stages of the employee lifecycle. Work with me to attract, hire, onboard, engage, perform, develop, and offboard with a clear vision and a shared commitment to excellence.

My method does not alter the order of the journey as presented earlier, because that is more or less what an individual goes through while in an organization's employment. However, I will expand on the employee engagement, performing, and developing stages. These stages are the longest and most ongoing phases of the employee lifecycle once a person starts working in a company. I have included unique flavors and combinations of the constructs of leadership, management, positive psychology, internal communication, rewards, recognition and pride, and wellbeing as major drivers of these critical aspects of the overall employee experience. My method offers a combination of best practices, personal experience, and well-researched techniques for attaining long-lasting engagement.

Additionally, I provide insights into how the performance and development journey of the employee can be shaped to yield better results. As for the remaining touchpoints—attracting, hiring, onboarding, offboarding—my fifteen-plus years of expertise in the field of employee experience will serve as an inspiration and a reference point.

Lastly, I stress the importance of constant, consistent evaluation of the segments of the employee experience. I provide a method for assessment and emphasize the significance of listening to employee voices and finding correlations between internal success and failure and how these affect customers externally.

Employees and customers are the foundation of any brand. By prioritizing their experiences, my method empowers employees to become an organization's strongest brand ambassadors, capable of creating robust, cohesive, dynamic, personal, transformative, and engaging experiences for customers. This will inspire customer loyalty and drive repeat business, all while building a strong and enduring brand.

My eX strategy requires collaboration with all stakeholders and is always subject to continuous evaluation and revision. Consistent feedback from a diverse range of stakeholders is vital, and taking swift action to enhance the experience is essential to maintain relevance. The unprecedented challenges brought about by the COVID-19 pandemic have shown us that organizations can adapt quickly, and agility is crucial in maintaining a world-class eX. With determination and a commitment to improvement, this signature eX method will set you apart from the competition.

Let's create a workplace where everyone plays a vital role in driving positive change. Always keep in mind the employees' core needs and align the eX to reflect the company's purpose, mission, and vision, as well as its employer brand, culture, and organizational identity. Let's embrace the significance of organizational values in shaping culture and commit to building a better tomorrow, starting today.

CHALLENGE ACCEPTED: PUTTING *THE EMPLOYEE JOURNEY* INTO ACTION

Here are some recommended activities. Remember to be creative, data-driven, and employee-centric, and tailor these tasks to your specific company culture and needs. By taking action and continuously iterating, you can build a truly unique and positive employee experience journey that attracts, engages, and retains top talent.

1. Hack Your Onboarding

Task: Reimagine your onboarding process to be more engaging and informative. Replace lengthy manuals with interactive training modules, gamified introductions, or buddy systems for instant connection.

Challenge: Identify three pain points in your current onboarding process that create confusion or frustration.

Activity: Brainstorm creative solutions to those pain points, focusing on personalized experiences. Think escape room–style team projects for learning key processes or scavenger hunts to introduce colleagues and company culture.

2. Map Your Employee Journey

Task: Using your current knowledge of the stages of the employee lifecycle (attracting, hiring, onboarding, engaging, performing, developing, departing), create a visual map of your company's employee journey.

Challenge: Identify three pivotal moments in the journey with the most potential for positive impact according to your company culture, keeping in mind the customer journey.

Activity: Organize creative brainstorming sessions to elevate these moments, incorporating surprise, recognition, or personalized elements, as discussed in this chapter. Develop strategies to make these moments memorable and positive. Consider incorporating elements of Pine and Gilmore's Four Realms or the value-creating opportunities framework to design a dramatic and transformative experience.

CHAPTER 5

A COMPANY CULTURE— INCEPTION, LIVING IT, AND TRANSFORMATIONS

"The culture of an organization is a reflection of the values, beliefs, and behaviors of the current leaders, and the institutional legacy of the values and beliefs of past leaders that have been institutionalized into the organization's structures, policies, and procedures."

—RICHARD BARRETT, FOUNDER OF
BARRETT VALUES CENTER

I absolutely love this quotation! It perfectly encapsulates the essence of culture. It highlights the significance of the leadership team in creating and driving the cultural journey. Additionally, it emphasizes that the entire organizational structure and its values play a crucial role in supporting culture. However, there is one crucial aspect I would like to add: It is not just senior leadership that shapes and propels the living company culture. The combined behavior of all employees is equally important. That being said, it is essential to acknowledge that senior leadership's involvement and full commitment to instilling culture is indispensable.

Many books, podcasts, and academic articles emphasize that an organization's core values are the foundation of its culture. A values-based framework is crucial in shaping, building, and driving culture, which are essential for achieving business success. However, things are never straightforward in reality, and many other factors come into play in shaping a company's evolving personality. This chapter will explore what it means to have a values-driven culture. We will discuss various aspects of daily life that may organically influence an organization's culture. Additionally, I will share my experiences with shaping and reshaping company culture.

When discussing the process of shaping an organization's culture, let's consider a few scenarios:

- a start-up or a new company, where the culture can be built from scratch
- a cultural transformation, where it is crucial to identify what works and what doesn't
- change management, mergers, and acquisitions, where a new culture can be created by combining old and new practices.

Regardless of the situation, reflection is important. Envision the way forward and engage key stakeholders in determining the best course of action. There is no one-size-fits-all approach to creating a thriving culture. Typically, companies start by identifying their vision and mission and then creating organizational values to help them achieve that vision. If executed with authenticity, meaning, and purpose, these values can lead companies toward greater productivity and profitability.

THE CORE VALUES

Organizations spend time developing core values, but do employees truly embody them? Do they only exist on paper?

Core values are the shared beliefs and commitments of an organization. They are the guiding principles that shape the company's culture and serve as its foundation. The ideal, easy-to-remember number of core values is typically between three and five. It is desirable for employees to feel proud of their core values and connect with them personally based on their own values and beliefs. Core values should reflect the DNA of the organization. I once worked at a company in Malta that had no sustainability strategy and neglected to protect the environment from its harmful emissions. This created a significant value conflict for me. On the other hand, with another employer in the UAE, everyone was encouraged to be creative, contribute with innovative ideas, and develop extraordinary solutions for clients. This was something that resonated deeply with me, and I felt a strong connection with that organization.

Values should not *only* be a set of principles hung up on the walls or mentioned on the company website. Values can be active elements of a company in a variety of ways. For example, applying cultural selection, psychometric assessments, and in-depth interviews during the recruitment process will ensure alignment with core values. This helps evaluate candidates based on their experience, attitude, beliefs, ethics, and values. By doing so, companies can connect with candidates over shared values and articulate what they stand for.

Further, coaching and training sessions should help employees understand why the core values are selected and how their roles help fulfill them and make a difference in customers' experiences. In official rewards and recognition programs, superstars should be selected because they live the company's core values, which should be embedded in policies, processes, and systems.

Values can be interwoven in written, verbal, and digital internal communications, such as surveys, town-hall meetings, and leadership talks. They can also be represented through visuals on walls, brochures, presentations, careers pages, company stationery, videos, and company theme songs. They can be shared digitally on the company intranet or the social media pages.

Authentic organizations reward or fire employees based on upholding or violating their core values. This is brave and genuine. The embodiment of the values can be assessed through performance management and performance appraisals. However, they must be observable and measurable, otherwise you can't know how well or how badly a person is doing.

Organizations must ensure that the external company brand is aligned with the desired internal culture and employee value proposition. This results in one clear, concise message and no disconnect between the internal and external brand and culture.

These are just a few examples of how you can bring a company's core values to life.

BEYOND THE CORE VALUES

In addition to a company's core values, there are a number of factors that influence and drive organizational culture, as represented in my list below. These aspects define the unique character and personality of an organization. If executed well, they ultimately contribute to a remarkable high-performance culture. They also make culture visible in daily interactions. Some of these factors are:

- an inspirational mission and vision
- an authentic and sustainable employee value proposition (EVP) and service philosophy
- appropriate physical and technological workspaces
- solid policies and standard operating procedures
- transparent and frequent internal communications—what *is* being said is just as important as what is *not* being said

- visible and respected internal survey scores that are acted upon
- a CSR strategy that is aligned with the culture
- diversity, inclusion, equity, equality, and belonging statements, practices, and policies
- encouragement and rewards for innovation
- a strategy rooted in learning, development, and growth opportunities
- a plan for celebration, appreciation, rewards, and recognition
- positive management and leadership styles; participation in company events
- a consistent corporate disciplinary process (the way mistakes are addressed)
- a representative selection process to attract candidates with the right culture and attitude fit
- clear guidelines for the way performance management is conducted
- treating new joiners and leavers with professionalism and care
- psychological safety, a climate of trust, and low levels of fear-based leadership to support low levels of cultural entropy
- ability to connect and develop meaningful relationships
- regular review of employee turnover rates to determine whether they're low, high, or healthy.

Although this list isn't exhaustive, it provides a guide to consider when creating or transforming an organizational culture.

For instance, it is crucial to acknowledge the EVP's importance and briefly touch on its development. This process requires research, feedback from interviews, and focus groups to put together an authentic proposition that employees feel part of. A value proposition that defines a company culture based on real-life feedback creates an extremely authentic representation of what an organization stands for and, in turn, attracts more people who are a good fit for the organization. Alignment of a company's core values, mission, vision, service philosophy, and employee value proposition creates internal cohesion. Internal cohesion is conducive to collective action.

Culture is a journey. It is not a place you arrive at overnight. With focused effort, it is a way of being that grows and improves over time.

SPREADING CULTURE

Preserving and maintaining culture is a responsibility that we (as employees) all share, but it must start from the top. To make a positive impact, leaders must be involved in the culture and be accessible to employees at all levels. Throughout my tenure at one of the largest resorts in the Middle East, several CEOs came and went. One individual made a significant impact by being present in people's lives. He would regularly have lunch at the colleague restaurant, sit next to different individuals each time, and discuss what worked and what didn't. He also encouraged his executive team to do the same, and soon SVPs and VPs who rarely ate at the restaurant began to genuinely show up and build relationships.

Culture starts from the top, but it trickles down through all layers of the organization. It also trickles back up and spreads horizontally. It is like the system of blood vessels, veins, and arteries in our bodies. Every individual is encouraged to interpret, embrace, and live it, especially if the culture is extraordinary and aligns with their personal beliefs. Earlier in this chapter, we looked at ways culture can spread. This included learning, development, and growth. Expertise in technical matters is essential, but understanding the company's culture is equally significant. Tailormade programs and opportunities that involve people in cultural development give it a unique voice. When there is an open and honest conversation, it begins to have a real impact. The company's culture is like a tree's root system. Every part of the roots helps to support the tree and is responsible for its flourishing. For this to happen, we must practice intentionality. We must nurture, water, prune, cut, and love the tree. This can be done via intentionally assigned tasks for people who add value with their contributions and help the culture grow positively.

Some of the most influential groups are the leadership and management team and the HR team. Then there are the unofficial cheerleaders who actively help develop and spread the culture throughout the organization. They do this by participating in company events and programs and encouraging others to join. Cheerleaders do not have to be loud. They can be quiet introverts who work from the back end. One of the best cheerleaders I have worked with is a Kenyan gentleman named Biko Ombete. Biko was initially a lifeguard and later became a scuba diver caring for the marine animals' habitat and environment. He was a quiet introvert who was revered in his community. If I needed to spread a message or look for volunteers, I sought him out. His personality and social stance were highly persuasive, and he was instrumental in touching the hearts and minds of many people.

Many companies have designated departments for culture. It is a necessity to have someone whose primary role is to oversee and track the culture strategy and development and drive it throughout the organization. Lately, some HR departments have started to change their names to "people and culture," but a name change is not enough. A complete paradigm shift needs to take place, especially in some organizations.

Furthermore, companies should put together a culture committee with official ambassadors and change champions who will promote company initiatives. I call these people "the custodians of culture." These passionate custodians have another central role, and that is to foster feedback through frequent dialogue. Ideally, they would possess critical skills and actively question something if it does not make sense. The custodians' impact is enormous, as they help communicate if teams do not adopt a program or a new policy well. I recommend training and empowering them to develop their capabilities as culture champions. This committee should hold quarterly meetings with a clear agenda and assigned responsibilities. One approach is to create a committee that includes representatives from different areas of the organization, with members rotating annually. The role of the committee and its members should also involve constructive criticism, where individuals are encouraged to apply critical thinking and, at times, act as the devil's advocate. This helps to prevent complacency and encourages challenging any status quo that may not be conducive to a remarkable and high-performance culture.

The phrase "this is the way" has gained popularity due to its use in the Disney+ TV series *The Mandalorian*. If you have watched the series, you know that Mandalorian culture is deeply rooted and preserved by its people. It requires a strong strategy, unwavering commitment, and integrity to uphold the traditions created by the Mandalorian ancestors.

OR ... OBLITERATING CULTURE?

When focusing on the benefits of a positive company culture with engaged employees, we must also address those who are feeling apathetic or disengaged. They pose unique challenges. I've observed that disengaged employees tend to become more vocal about their dissatisfaction with the company, even before they resign or during their notice period. This negative attitude can spread to others who feel similarly disconnected, leading to a prolonged period of discontentment that can affect the entire team. Encourage open communication with these individuals to address their challenges.

Not everyone will fully embrace and connect with a company's culture, since no culture suits every employee. Some employees may not be on board with the culture but nevertheless surpass their goals. If a particular leader is not on board with the culture, their team may be ill-informed about specific programs. In this case, they create their own subcultures, which may deviate far from the company's. This is particularly evident in multinational organizations, where the culture is also shaped by the diverse local cultures of the employees working there. In one multicultural organization where I worked, the head of one department was kind but ruled with an iron fist. He and his entire team were all the same gender and from the same country in Asia. Their annual colleague engagement scores were always 100%, while the rest of the departments—which had a vast mix of nationalities, ethnicities, and genders—rarely achieved 100%. Naturally, the HR department was curious about how his department achieved perfect scores and how he successfully maintained them. We wanted to build a best-case practice and see if this could help other departments with less engaged employees. When we dug deep, we found out that the employees from that particular country were raised to never to question the leader and always be grateful for what is given to them. There was also an element of fear entangled with admiration. There was very little that members of this department wanted because they felt a duty to their leader and were grateful that he had given them a job. There was also little growth and almost no expression of individuality. While the department mostly achieved its goals and exhibited perfect engagement on paper, you can conclude how engaged people truly were.

By staying connected to subcultures, leaders and HR teams can ensure that the overall company culture is aligned and foster an environment of growth and collaboration.

Though everyone plays a role in shaping and improving culture, one person in a position of power can destroy it entirely. Workplace psychopaths in leadership positions can be exceptionally dangerous and toxic to culture. I have personally witnessed this happen in my career. Seeing how an individual's actions could dismantle a culture of trust, empowerment, and loyalty was horrifying. If we had measured the levels of cultural entropy while they were employed, they would have been alarmingly high. There was very little psychological safety. We experienced high degrees of dysfunction, friction, and frustration. Many people around them acted out of fear and inauthenticity. They created anxiety, were manipulative, and were quick to fire good people. This individual's behavior was comparable to Daenerys' actions in the final episode of the award-winning series *Game of Thrones*, wherein she ruthlessly torched King's Landing and its people with her dragons. While some individuals escaped the destruction, those who remained suffered long-term scars.

HOW DO YOU MEASURE CULTURE? WHAT DO YOU DO ABOUT YOUR FINDINGS?

There are several ways to measure cultural health and cultural entropy (friction, fear, and frustration), which are discussed in the Metrics chapter. Ultimately, it is about giving employees a voice. These measurements may be communicated to the organization in an annual culture report to create a shared picture from data collection and dialogue. This way, the organization can follow the cultural journey and transformation (if applicable) and feel part of it.

A combination of quantitative and qualitative research is advisable. The former could be a cultural assessment survey, where I advise aiming for 80–100% participation. I know this is hard in some organizations, especially those whose reputation for acting on the results is abysmal. Sadly, many of these organizations won't admit it, or perhaps don't know how to fix it. But this is another topic for another book. The survey needs a high participation rate from all demographics for it to be inclusive and meaningful. The latter would be qualitative and involve focus groups or interviews.

In the earlier days of my career, while working at a large organization, we faced a significant cultural crisis. Our annual employee engagement survey revealed that many of the employees were dissatisfied with their work. They cited several reasons, including a lack of work-life balance due to long hours. There were also issues with new rosters being communicated at the last minute, long periods on the night shift, and expectations for employees to respond to their phones or emails while they were off or on leave. The survey also showed that there was a big issue with psychological safety, as trust levels had significantly dropped compared to previous years. At the same time, we found out that our employer brand was not well-regarded. To make things worse, we had a growing percentage of employees leaving, which led to high employee turnover costs.

We were not the first and wouldn't be the last organization to go through a cultural crisis. When we started to analyze the root causes, we found that some of them were external.

WHAT DID WE DO?

We scheduled a mandatory meeting with all managers and senior leaders. We engaged in a long and detailed workshop where all cards came out on the table, and the result was a list of approximately thirty things that we, as managers and leaders, would *stop* doing and another thirty things we would *start* doing. We communicated our intentions to the rest of the organization and asked them to vote for their top ten dos and don'ts. As an HR team, we then turned the most popular choices into a cultural statement called "The Ten Commandments." These were visually displayed in the employee-only areas. Departments were encouraged to select the 'do' they most resonated with and participate in a painting competition. Each participating department had a piece of that wall, a canvas that was approximately two meters long and two meters tall. They used their talent to display what the selected statement meant to them and how they interpreted it. This competition and cultural activation journey took a year to complete. The crowning of a winner was a big day in the organization. Competing departments visited offices to campaign for their artwork. The department with the best campaign had dressed in unique t-shirts and funky hats, and carried whistles, creating a lot of attention and excitement around their artwork. The winner was a secondary matter; what was central was the journey the organization went through. Not every department took part, but everyone passed by that long wall and was reminded daily of our commitment as a team.

Simultaneously, the L&D department launched a five-module cultural training course for all managers and senior leaders. As an HR team, we conducted structural realignment to our core values and mission statement. We stepped back, re-evaluated, and reconfigured structures, policies, procedures, and incentives. The executive team also made critical changes to their morning briefings. We had a few problematic leaders who did not fit the newly created culture, and I was told "We will either change them or change them." It took a couple of seconds before that sank in. Eventually, we did end up changing them.

This worked for us, but there are so many other roadmaps that companies can embark on when transforming their culture. The essential elements are:

- regular assessment of the culture, the changes, the progress, and the impact of these changes

- personal and collective commitment from the leadership team
- continuous, consistent, and intentional listening to understand, align, and not blame
- compassion and kindness
- involving different people in shaping culture and engaging all voices.

Another way your organization can build its desired workplace culture is through the Culture Design Canvas Framework developed by Gustavo Razzetti. It's like a blueprint that breaks culture down into nine essential elements, providing a practical approach to shaping and achieving your ideal work environment.

Using the framework, teams can collaboratively:

- identify their desired culture
- diagnose current culture
- develop action plans
- track progress and adapt.

A third framework that I particularly like is David Friedman's Culture by Design, which he succinctly explains in his book and course *Culture by Design: How to Build a High-Performing Culture, Even in the New Remote Work Environment*. His teachings provide a structured approach to assessing, designing, and implementing a desired organizational culture. The framework utilizes key elements like values, practices, rituals, and structures to guide culture-building efforts.

One thing to note is that a cultural journey never ends; it continues to evolve organically.

A SENSE OF BELONGING

Although a company may have an incredible mission statement, inspiring vision, and genuine core values and practices, it may not be sufficient for employees to feel included. The company's core values must align with employees' values to establish a genuine connection. This allows the individual to embody the company's culture and live it authentically and with a sense of loyalty.

On another recent occasion, as a consultant, I organized a town-hall meeting for the entire organization. The CEO spoke at this event. There were approximately eight hundred people present. His topic was 'quality.' As he passionately described what it meant to give and show quality to clients and how employees' actions resulted in the personal success of customers, one bellman sitting at the front of the room indicated that he wanted to ask a question. The bellman stood up, took his shoe off, and showed it to the CEO. He took the microphone and bravely asked how he expected employees to demonstrate quality if the shoes given as part of the uniform were ripped open and the soles gaped at him. The stunned silence followed by loud applause indicated the sentiment that people in the room felt. Within the same month, the issue with uniforms and shoes was resolved and a process for further continuous improvement was implemented.

It is not enough to talk about a culture of quality for customers when the employees themselves are not given quality. This doesn't help to develop a sense of belonging or authenticity. Instead, an environment that has integrity, fosters trust and facilitates the development of meaningful connections between co-workers must be nurtured to create a place where people feel they belong.

AND THE JOURNEY BEGINS ...

The culture of a company has a direct impact on the experiences of its employees, which ultimately affects the experiences of customers. All the elements that make up the company culture play a crucial role in shaping the overall experiences of employees and customers. The leaders who truly understand this correlation are busy building and sustaining a culture that consistently outperforms the competition. Those who do not are encouraged to take inspiration from this book and anything else that inspires them.

Let's look at how this is done by delving into the first stage of the employee lifecycle. I have combined the *attract*, *identify*, *hire*, and *onboard* aspects into one chapter. Welcome on board!

CHALLENGE ACCEPTED: PUTTING *CULTURE FORMATION* INTO ACTION

Here are some recommended activities you can do after having read this chapter. The key is to make these tasks actionable, engaging, and measurable. I encourage you to actively participate in shaping your company culture.

1. Culture Design Canvas Challenge

Task: Gather your team and create a visual map of your company's desired culture using the "Culture Design Canvas" framework.

Challenge: Discuss and define each element, ensuring every person has a voice in shaping your ideal culture.

Activity: Display your completed work prominently as a constant reminder of your shared aspirations and a roadmap for future actions. Align the culture work with everything related to the company and make it come to life.

2. "Values in Action" Showcase

Task: Individuals nominate colleagues who exemplify your company's values through their actions and contributions.

Challenge: They must then highlight specific examples of how these values manifest in everyday work.

Activity: Create a public "Values Wall" featuring photos and descriptions of the nominated individuals, celebrating their positive impact on the culture.

3. "Reverse Mentorship Lunch"

Task: Pair senior employees with junior colleagues for informal lunch meetings.

Challenge: Encourage senior employees to learn fresh perspectives and ideas from their junior counterparts.

Activity: Focus on open dialogue and knowledge exchange, fostering cross-generational connection and a more inclusive culture.

PART 2 Let the Adventure Begin

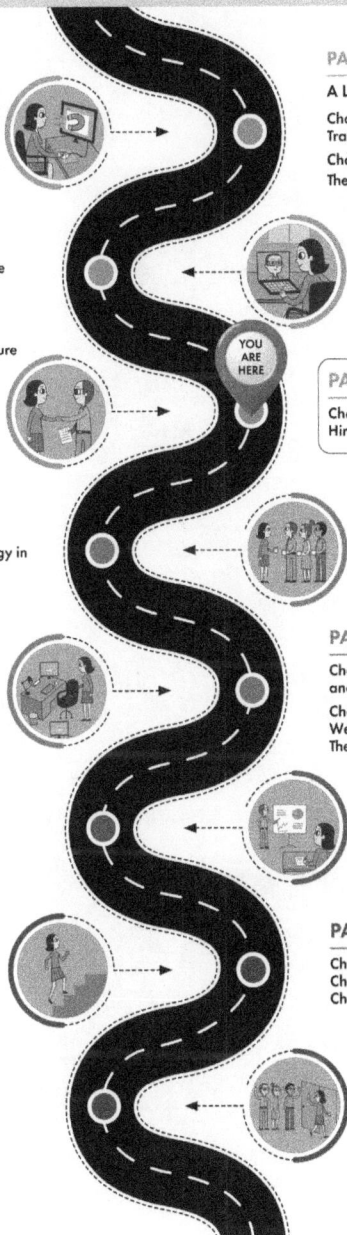

YOU ARE HERE

CHAPTER 6

ATTRACT, IDENTIFY, HIRE, ONBOARD

Once upon a time, there lived a little blond girl who was almost called Augustina. Interestingly, her mother had contemplated naming her Augustina to commemorate the day of her birth—August 31st. Like other little girls and boys around her, she possessed her own unique magical powers. From a young age, she was a remarkable creature driven by a powerful sense of purpose and a fierce determination to achieve her goals—so much so that the adults around her nicknamed her 'The Iron Lady' after Margaret Thatcher. Her commitment to being mischievous and having fun and her relentless pursuit of excellence set her apart from her friends. She was widely admired and respected for her outstanding scholastic achievements and unwavering dedication to her dreams. Despite the challenges she faced along the way, the little girl refused to give up, and she remained steadfast in her pursuit of greatness, inspiring others to follow in her footsteps and reach for the stars.

As she grew, she became a youthful and vibrant lady with an insatiable curiosity about the world around her. One day, on a cool but sunny afternoon on the Mediterranean island of Malta, she witnessed a memorable and inspiring sight: a group of dazzling ladies dressed in distinctive beige and red costumes with elegant hats adorned with long, silky veils. Each lady had a petite suitcase, and one could imagine it brimming with an array of unimaginable goodies from faraway lands! They all looked beautifully styled, and their bright red lipstick was the envy of every lady (and some gentlemen) in town. These women quickly disappeared from her sight, and it was a long time until she saw them again. This time, she was determined to understand who these mysterious, attractive goddesses were. With trepidation, she cautiously approached them, her heart beating faster as they revealed who they were. They were the flight attendants of Emirates Airlines, flying to a far-away land called the United Arab Emirates, where sheiks and princesses lived.

From that moment on, the only thing that 'almost Augustina' could think about was how she could join their exclusive club. With her natural inquisitiveness and perseverance, she discovered more about their existence, collected tales of their whereabouts, and established relationships with a chosen few. Everything that people whispered about them was fantastical. This is all she could think and dream about. She became possessed. And, as luck would have it, one day she also flew to the United Arab Emirates. Thanks to her diligent efforts and commitment, she was granted the honor of being invited to participate in an interview for membership in their prestigious club. She prepared for this special day with anticipation, carefully reading all the instructions and information to help her become 'a chosen one.' She memorized what they stood for, their beliefs, and their aspirations. But sadly, it was not meant to be, and a heartbroken 'almost Augustina' closed that chapter of her magical fairytale life and moved on to even more exciting feats.

This little girl was, in fact, me.

And even though I never received the opportunity to join Emirates Airlines as cabin crew, I made it a point to fly Emirates whenever possible! Their reputation as employers and their stories from travels around the world continue to inspire thousands of people to join their organization every day. They continue to be innovators in employee work practices. This is a fabulous example of a solid and influential employer brand. How do they do it? Why do they do it?

Let's delve into the first touchpoint of an employee's journey. From a company's perspective, this usually begins with the following:

1. creating awareness about their company and attracting talented candidates
2. identifying, sourcing, interviewing, shortlisting, hiring, and pre-boarding selected superstars
3. onboarding and welcoming them to the organization.

People commonly think that recruiting and onboarding an employee only takes a few months, completely disregarding the work companies do in the background to create a reputation as an employer of choice and to develop, improve, and uphold this reputation. It is as important as the brand's reputation. Companies spend thousands and millions on marketing and PR to attract potential clients and retain current ones. They may spend equally large sums to attract and retain potential employees. The employer brand is created and supported by a recruitment marketing and an employee advocacy strategy, a budget, and a company's commercial brand. These go hand in hand, and the complex relationship between them may sometimes be misleading. For instance, many famous companies have excellent commercial brands but could do better as employers. This might be because they don't have an employer branding strategy and fail to invest enough in the entirety of the employee experience.

This chapter began with a story from my early twenties. The Emirates Airlines fairytale took place when I was twenty-three. By the time I had an interview with them, I was twenty-six! That was three years of me, as a potential employee, being attracted, kept interested, and eventually invited for an interview. The deliberate work companies do to attract potential candidates is vital to an organization's talent pool. A great employer brand can take several years to build and a lifetime to sustain.

So, does the employer brand really matter? Companies are constantly competing to attract and hire exceptional talent, and if your reputation as an employer is weak, you will not be people's first choice when they apply for jobs. However, that's not the only reason. The external employer brand affects the overall employee experience, engagement, motivation, and sense of pride. If you work in a company that is externally perceived as an ethical employer that does excellent work, your trust levels as an employee are more likely to be high and you (and your loved ones) will be proud of your workplace. The entirety of Chapter Ten is dedicated to motivation, pride, rewards, and recognition, demonstrating these concepts' importance in the employee journey.

Another crucial reason to strategize and execute a professional employer brand is to reduce risk to your business. When starting my consultancy career, I worked with a client with a terrible employer brand. Headhunted candidates were declining job offers, and suppliers would not actively choose to work with them. Even more mortifyingly, customers heard stories about the mistreatment of their employees (from the employees themselves) and wrote about it in the newspapers! Who wants to use the services of a company known for unethical employer practices? This is why the employer brand matters. It matters a lot.

A negative candidate experience or a substandard employee experience can harm your employer brand in the same way that bad publicity can damage your corporate brand. Support from leadership, as well as consistent attention, investment, and measurement, are necessary to build and maintain a thriving employer brand.

Attracting employees to join a company can be done through several direct and indirect approaches, such as the ones presented in the following table.

Table 1. Attracting Potential Employees

Media Influence	Physical Presence		Advocacy
Attractive and inspiring company social media content, useful topics discussed in blogs, etc. Well-designed and informative company website and career sites. The more social engagement with posts or the career site, the more popular the brand.	A well-organized and professional presence at company recruitment fairs. Keep in mind that whatever you do, the industry itself or the nature of the job can attract or deter people from joining a company. E.g., people who are against smoking may not want to join a company that manufactures cigarettes.	A positive contribution to the environment and society through CSR events and sustainability activities. People with altruistic traits may prefer to work at a company that contributes to the improvement of the environment or their community. Community outreach such as volunteering to assist or organize meaningful events.	Employees and ex-employees saying positive and inspirational things about the company spreads like wildfire. However, employees may also say negative things, which could deter potential candidates.

Media Influence	Physical Presence		Advocacy
Career portals with up-to-date vacancies; career sites like LinkedIn and Glassdoor demonstrating diverse and inclusive hiring practices.	Inspirational intern and graduate trainee events/programs; visits to schools, colleges, and universities where individuals can be attracted to apply.	The way employees physically look, dress, behave, and perform can influence people to find out more about the company and possibly apply.	Friends and family of employees and ex-employees saying great things about the company builds a sense of trust and pride for current employees and potential candidates.
Recruitment and headhunting agencies that talk positively about an organization and have merchandise from the company that they can showcase or give away.	Sponsorship of popular sports events, e.g., FIFA, World Cup, Superbowl, Cricket Cups, Olympics, etc. where potential employees can find out about the brand.	Participating in external industry awards such as Top Employer, Great Place to Work and being ISO, LEED, and WELL certified etc. shows possible candidates that the workplace cares for employee wellbeing.	Clients/ consultants who love working with the company so much that they decide to become employees. This sends a clear positive message.

Media Influence	Physical Presence		Advocacy
Traditional media, newspapers, TV shows, etc. that mention the company in a positive light.	Participating in conferences, podcasts, and workshops that talk about employee practices.	Participating in company-related sports events with strong teams and winning awards. Competitors will know the company for having talented employees/ contestants.	Success stories from employees about personal and professional growth and work promotions. These indicate the company focuses on developing their people and possibly their family members too.
Books and magazines that mention the company in a positive light.	Sponsoring talented individuals to finish training/ degrees for a profession needed in their company with a guarantee of employment once they graduate.	Recruitment marketing strategies that focus on attracting the right people for the right reasons; transparency and equity in salaries and benefits.	Customers talking about the level of professionalism and knowledge that employees have.

The examples in the table above can inspire your own employer branding strategy.

I invite you to consider what your company does to create a positive employer brand. Are you proud? Can you do better? When was the last time you checked your reputation as an employer? Think about the impact of not having a strategy.

Specialized organizations conduct research, both qualitative and quantitative, with random samples of non-employees to understand a company's employer brand. For a sample of a typical survey, please visit my website (www.beyond-employeeengagement.com) and download a free copy. I have included several other metrics for employer branding in Chapter 14.

When a company positively captures someone's attention, it opens up a world of possibilities. Even if that person doesn't end up joining the team, the seed of inspiration has been planted. And, if they do decide to apply for a vacancy, they embark on the next step of the journey.

The next section delves into the essential touchpoints of clarity, ease, and speed in the job application process; the professionalism exhibited during the interview; and the job offer or rejection. Each of these touchpoints carries equal weight and gives individuals an idea of what they can expect if they join an organization.

THE CANDIDATE IS INTERESTED. WHAT NEXT?

How many times have you applied for a job online and gotten frustrated with the length of the application process? Most of us simply want to upload a CV and click *submit*! Instead, some companies require you to go through a cumbersome process of creating a profile (with ridiculous password requirements) before you even have the opportunity to submit your application. Worse, some career sites are not mobile-friendly and must be navigated with a desktop or laptop. What if the candidate doesn't have one?

What if they are on their phone sitting on the metro when they decide to apply? I used to work with an inspirational leader who always focused on delivering top quality. He was famous for the phrase "Everything considered." This means that every tiny detail of the employee and the customer journey must be considered if your organization is to stand out from the competition.

At this stage of the journey, the employee experience is heavily influenced by the technological environment. This includes how accessible and up-to-date your career site is. I once worked at a large company that did not have a careers site for many years. People would contact me directly to ask what job openings we had, as there was very little visibility and accessibility. Needless to say, it did not give a good impression. Instead, the company hired mostly through recruitment agencies, walk-ins, referrals, and mass career fairs. To be fair, it worked. It worked well. But I often wonder how sustainable this would have been under different circumstances, or how much better the employer brand could have been if there was a quality careers page.

I recommend removing digital friction as much as possible in accordance with your budget. This requires flawless collaboration between HR and IT. Ensure that your company career page is user-friendly, reliable, sustainable, updated, inspirational, and tells your company story. Once you've perfected that, it's time to focus on every other job-hosting platform. Establish agreements with recruitment agencies, educational bodies, government institutions, ministries, and embassies. You might wonder why I suggest government institutions.

In a previous company, we hired approximately fifty talented individuals from a small nation called Bhutan. This was a very rare opportunity for Bhutanese people to work outside of their country, and it was a strategic decision to encourage their employment so they could be trained internationally and improve their English. The opportunity was significant for the country, so much so that Bhutan's princess visited them and inquired about their wellbeing and professional development. We experienced similar situations with China and the Philippines, where their ambassadors were heavily involved with the sourcing, interviewing, recruitment, placement, and overall welfare of their people. This was highly beneficial for diversity and inclusion and helped tremendously with our recruitment marketing strategy. Networking and connections—that's what we were known for.

Once you have perfected the workflows, processes, and digital employee experience so candidates can apply for jobs easily, I recommend getting your external communication right. This includes all the auto-generated messages such as 'Thank you for applying for this position,' 'You have been shortlisted for an online interview,' and even the dreaded 'Unfortunately, you have not been selected.' You could be looking at thirty to fifty different types of communication. Make sure to pre-script them and use your brand values to ascertain that people are having a good experience with your employer brand. Make no mistake: End users read these messages and form opinions about your brand.

Finding the right cultural fit is crucial to the success of the hiring process and the longevity and productivity of employees. You often hear recruiters or leaders say they hire for attitude rather than skill. Well, putting interviewees in the position to be their best is a skill. How an interview is conducted can bring out the worst or the best in a candidate, and it can speak volumes about your employer brand. As I was preparing to write this chapter, I received a call from a close friend who wanted to share about a job interview she'd had that day. The first red flag was that both the interviewers logged on for the online interview seven minutes late. One interviewer had her camera on, but the other one didn't. The interview lasted for fifteen minutes, and the visible interviewer was typing something on her phone most of the time. My friend described it as the worst interview she'd had in her entire career, and she said that she had logged off feeling like her accomplishments were not good enough for the people interviewing her. People who go through such an experience may not even consider a second interview if the company offers one. This is how quickly you can lose a great candidate, unless you pay very well—but then people may want to join for the wrong reasons! You can see how failing to train the recruitment team is a recipe for disaster. Richard Branson famously says, "Train people well enough so they can leave, treat them well enough so they don't want to." This advice applies to all employees, but in this initial stage recruiters play a big role in representing the company. One of the most crucial aspects of a recruitment strategy is creating an outstanding interview process. Consider some of these essential touchpoints:

- Was interview booking done professionally, and were candidates given several suitable dates/times? Were they provided with necessary details such as the interview location (or an online link) ahead of time? Did they know who would be conducting the interview? If headhunted, were they provided a job description?
- Was the recruiter on time and well-prepared regarding the candidate's CV and achievements? Sometimes, you can see recruiters scanning a CV for the first time during the interview and asking shallow questions.

- Talking about questions, does your company have a set reper-
toire for interviews? When I was working at Aldar Properties in
Abu Dhabi, I liked to meet the candidates at the ground floor
reception, take them upstairs to the rooftop, show them our ter-
race, gym, and yoga studio, and then take them down to the
interview room. This broke the ice and inspired candidates to
want to work there. I would even use this walk to assess their
ability to take notice, to connect, and to communicate with others. The process might be a little lengthy, but this is a vital touchpoint in the employee experience, and it must be conducted
professionally.

- Some follow-up interviews require a computer skills test, while
others require that practical skills, such as those of a chef, be
assessed. How well-prepared and organized is the recruiter
for this? Is the hiring manager there on time to meet and assess
the candidate?

- Will you use psychometric assessments? If yes, how will the
candidate benefit from this? If employed, will the candidate be
walked through their assessment results? Will this be used as
the foundation of a personal development plan?

- If a candidate is unsuccessful, how soon will you inform them?
Do you take three months? Do you ghost them? How do you
let them know in such a way that they walk away from the
experience as brand advocates?

There are many details to consider and prepare for while interviewing and hiring. The next part of the employee journey is pre-
boarding. This is when the candidate has accepted the job offer
and begun the process of document provision, resignation, and
all other formalities involved in changing companies, embarking

on their first job, or even relocating to another country. Once again, technology plays a vital role in the smooth flow of the pre-boarding documents collection process. This is all part of the digital employee experience (DeX). When it comes to pre-boarding, there are several other aspects to consider. It's not just about document collection.

According to a survey conducted by CareerBuilder and Silkroad Technology, one in ten employees have left a company because of a poor onboarding experience, and 37% of those interviewed said that their manager did not play a critical role in their onboarding experience. Without a proper pre-boarding process, the chances of employees quitting before they even join increases. Employee turnover and loss of productivity also increase. According to a writeup in the *Harvard Business Review*, 33% of new hires begin to look for a different job within the first six months of joining a new organization. Sadly, about half of my clients faced this challenge. I often found myself creating inclusive and engaging onboarding strategies involving managers and leaders. From my consultancy experience, this issue is often seen in start-ups and companies in their early stages that are too focused on growth, expansion, and making money, so managers have very little time to be part of their new employees' onboarding experience. Thus, it's essential to emphasize the significance of regular, candid, and open communication with new employees and their managers. Building a connection and fostering a two-way relationship is crucial during the pre-boarding and onboarding processes, and the hiring manager and the recruiter play a significant role in that.

In addition to human interaction, technology is also necessary. There are digital solutions with dedicated modules for pre-boarding and onboarding. This is the company's chance to further showcase the employer brand and get people excited about joining. The HR team could use this technology to:

- automatically send a pre-boarding invitation with an agenda
- send out a company intro and welcome video from the leaders and/or the hiring manager/host department
- personalize the onboarding experience for different levels of employees in different departments
- provide an introduction to and training about the company mission and core values, setting expectations for what's to come
- host a centralized space for onboarding material, FAQs, and live chats with company onboarding ambassadors
- allow new employees to network in the same 'space' and get to know each other long before they join
- provide an introduction to organizational culture
- share schedules for company orientation and departmental orientation, with calendar invites for interviews with key leaders
- share IT information, updates, and systems training, setting the tone for a positive DeX
- send out prerequisite training, such as the company's code of business conduct or diversity training
- provide necessary checklists and process maps for what is to be completed before Day 1.

An excellent pre-boarding experience is created by balancing human and digital interaction.

The last touchpoint of the *attract, identify, hire, onboard* stage of the employee journey commences when the employee officially begins their first day at work. That's the onboarding. In the next section, we will discuss what kind of experience you can create for new employees, which can inspire them to create amazing experiences for customers.

ONBOARDING: COMPANY AND DEPARTMENTAL ORIENTATION

A good onboarding program could last up to one year. While researching this chapter, I realized that what I considered a basic onboarding and first-week orientation program was something many people had not experienced in their companies. I once worked at an organization where new employees began work at any time and would not attend company orientation until a few weeks or even months later. By the time this occurred, they'd already learned what they needed to know on their own. One of the first changes I made as VP of employee experience was to limit onboarding to twice a month on pre-selected dates. New employees' first week would be solely dedicated to onboarding and orientation.

My recommended process creates a much-needed connection. It opens the employee's experience on the job with an inspirational, educational, immersive company orientation. The new employee experiences a transformational journey and gains a more in-depth cultural understanding of how the company makes money. This makes for a smooth entry into their department, and employees generally feel more equipped to begin work. By beginning with a planned orientation, HR stages and controls the narrative and the experience.

A comprehensive orientation, which may take a week, would include the following:

- company information, mission, culture pillars, and long-term roadmap
- inspirational content that makes new employees proud of current achievements and the company's future strategy
- a good overview of key departments and how they work together
- a segment where HR explains the value and services they provide to all
- fun and interactive training on the company's core values and what makes them who they are
- IT setup (if necessary)
- a tour of the office/premises, other buildings, or assets owned by the company (can be done virtually if necessary); companies can also use VR technology that allows new employees to choose their avatar and explore the entirety of the company portfolio with an interactive voiceover
- organizational culture should shine throughout orientation; this can include icebreakers, opportunities for networking, establishing genuine connections, meeting new people, and getting to know about the experiences of current employees
- team-building events focused on organizational values for greater immersion
- ample opportunities for human connection, interaction, and feedback
- leadership involvement, ideally physically, or virtually if necessary; coming to present at Orientation and establishing a connection with new joiners from the onset, or at the very least,

provide a creative welcome video where leaders express their appreciation to the new employees for joining the company

- wellness program overview
- intranet overview, including downloading the app (or any apps that are integral to the employee experience) and demonstrating its functions live so employees know where to find key information
- sharing employee activities/events/sports groups/CSR groups which may be of interest to them to join and help them feel like part of a community.

At one of my workplaces, the last day of the week-long orientation focused on fun, kindness, connection, and giving back. The new employees were given the opportunity to pair up during the beginning of orientation, and they had an entire week to create something for their partner, showcasing their unique talents. The last day was a celebration of their gifts and a show of appreciation from one new employee to another. We had people reciting poems, singing songs, and dancing for their partners. We even had someone prepare a special dessert and a DJ jamming to the new employee's favorite music while showing a video of pictures taken throughout orientation. It truly showcased the type of culture we had built. The new employees' managers were also invited to watch this last segment and would then take them to their workstations and show them around before they began work the following Monday.

Tailoring orientation to the employee's role is essential for making employees at every level of the company feel valued. By providing tailored training, new hires can feel confident and prepared to excel. New managers can benefit from training sessions on the company culture, employee engagement, performance management, and various HR and IT systems. Meanwhile, entry-level employees can focus on customer service and service recovery. Interns, fresh graduates, contractors, part-time and seasonal workers, and consultants also have unique training needs that must be considered. Providing personalized touches, such as serving their favorite beverage on their first day or providing creative welcome gifts and personalized table placements, can make all the difference. All these little touches and details make the difference between average and extraordinary.

The next part of onboarding could last three to six months, sometimes longer depending on the length of the probation period. This is the time for meaningfully connecting with co-workers and leaders and truly understanding the culture. During this time, managers must set up regular meetings with the new joiners and participate in their journey by supporting them, empowering them, and setting clear goals and expectations. Some companies use psychometric tests throughout the recruitment process. Managers may wish to discuss the test results and set a path forward for the new joiner to utilize their strengths. A little later, the L&D team should also discuss the employee's initial training needs and develop a learning journey to help them thrive and grow.

Awesome workplaces usually have a buddy system: someone outside the HR team is assigned to help the new joiner fit in while allowing their individuality to shine. The buddy typically has regular lunches/break times with the new employee and helps them get immersed in the unspoken company culture. Buddies must be selected and trained to be part of this planned professional experience. It is recommended that the new joiner attend company events to connect with people in a different setting and get to know them better. This is crucial to establishing a good network.

Connections at work are everything. Without connections, there is no sense of belonging. Without a sense of belonging, employees quietly quit and sometimes leave the organization.

The next few months are when a new employee begins to feel comfortable in an organization, like a newly planted tree beginning to feel its way around the garden and eventually starting to conquer ground and spread roots. The tree requires sunshine and good-quality soil with plenty of nutrients and water. The tree requires kindness, attention, and love to flourish and produce flowers or fruits. How are you facilitating this in your garden (i.e., your department)?

I have put together a roadmap to introduce this figure as it defines the touchpoints along an employee journey. I have broken the journey into attracting, recruiting, onboarding, engaging, developing, performing, departing, and potentially reboarding. This roadmap can be referred to as many times as required, and I invite you to visit my website (www.beyond-employeeengagement.com) to take a closer and more detailed look at the various stages.

THE EMPLOYEE JOURNEY

STEP 1: ATTRACTING AND PRE-BOARDING

INFORMING

Building Brand Awareness
Strategizing & Executing Employer Branding
Recruitment Marketing
Consider multiple personas; emphasize D,E&I

**GENERATING
A LEAD**

Website & Career Page
Recruitment Platforms
Recruitment Agencies
Social Media Channels
Job Fairs
Headhunting
Direct applicants
Employee Referral Program

**LEAD
CONSIDERATION**

The Organization's Signature Recruitment Style
Sourcing and Screening
Candidate Preparation: Sneak Peak of Interview Structure
Scoring & Reviewing Candidates
Interviews Style with set questions and scripts
Organized calls
Calendar Invitations with necessary details
Personal and Automated Messages
Showcase Employee Value Proposition
Conversations & Culture Transference
Psychometric Assessments for Org. Values & Case Studies
Interview Feedback
Involvement of Hiring Managers: custodians of culture
Mini Office Tour if applicable (physical, virtual, via metaverse)

**CONVERTING
A LEAD AND
VALUE DELIVERY**

Negotiation and Closing
Acceptance
Company Concierge for city tour, housing, schools, hospitals
Congratulate new hire
Pre-boarding
Documents collection
The beginning of value delivery
Organization announces new hire
Agenda for the first week
Toolkits Preparation: HR, IT, Security: workstation, PC, ID Card, etc

THE EMPLOYEE JOURNEY

STEP 2: BRAND ADVOCACY & ONBOARDING

WEEK 1

The Official Immersion in the Company Experience Company
Orientation & Necessary Training tailored to personas
PC setup, printer, software, uniform, tools, office access
In-depth Office Tour, including assets, different buildings, etc
Team building with other new joiners (if applicable)
Initiative: Show kindness to someone
Manager shows new joiner the official workplace (if applicable)
Administering Experience Survey

WEEK 2 & 3

Department Orientation
Entry Interview: What the new joiner needs to succeed
Individual Ergonomic Assessment & Training - onboarding related to
use of special desks
Meeting your team & Manager to network
Discussion of psychometric assessment (if applicable)
Set up a plan for regular meetings with the manager and team
Setting Probation Goals & KPIs
Begin daily work tasks and meet new people
Understand people, processes, and systems
Meeting key stakeholders to network
Introduction to Cultural Buddy
Attend necessary training (virtual or in-person)
Initiative: Show kindness to someone; practice empathy
Continue meeting stakeholders and understand company culture
Spend time in different departments to understand the business

DAYS 30

Monthly meeting with Employee Experience team
Official meeting with Department Head
Training Needs Analysis and Job Training Discussions
Review the progress of Probation Goals
Training & on-the-job experience
Continuation of Culture Immersion
Attend two official company events to network
Meeting with key departments (IT, Finance, etc.)
Orientation Reunion with HR team to discuss experience
Initiative: Submit Innovation/Improvement Suggestion
Tea with the CEO/GM
Cross Exposure in different departments (for interns/trainees)
Initiative: Show appreciation and kindness to someone
Administering Experience Survey

THE EMPLOYEE JOURNEY

STEP 2: BRAND ADVOCACY & ONBOARDING

DAYS 60

Strengths-focused chat with the manager
Review of probation goals
Training & on-the-job experience
Attend two official company events to network
Product Orientation continued if necessary
Meet with stakeholders and learn about their processes
Initiative: Volunteering Experience
Continuation of Culture Immersion
Initiative: Show appreciation and recognition to someone

DAYS 90

Review Probation Goal
Confirmation of Employment or Extension of Probation
End of Buddy Program
Update LinkedIn status and work experience
Leave a Glassdoor review
Continue Employee Advocacy
Set annual KPIs
Training & on-the-job experience
Departmental Team Building
Attend two official company events and connect with new people
Set up official regular meetings with Department Head
Initiative: Show appreciation and kindness to someone
Initiative: Suggestion one improvement/innovative idea

DAYS 180

Probation discussion: employment confirmation or end of employment
Career Discussion
Individual and Professional Development Plan
Training & on-the-job experience
Initiative: Show appreciation to someone
Initiative: Show kindness to someone
Attend two company events to network
Administering Experience Survey

THE EMPLOYEE JOURNEY

STEP 3: THE JOURNEY BEYOND PROBATION

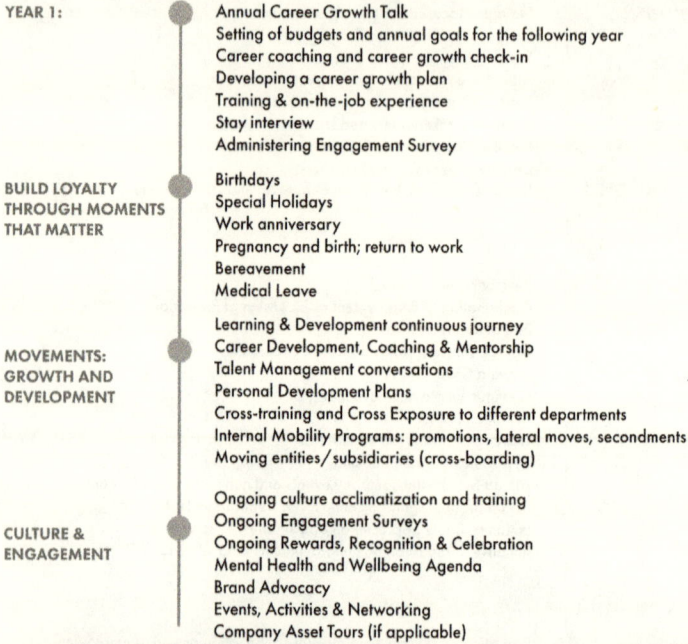

YEAR 1:
- Annual Career Growth Talk
- Setting of budgets and annual goals for the following year
- Career coaching and career growth check-in
- Developing a career growth plan
- Training & on-the-job experience
- Stay interview
- Administering Engagement Survey

BUILD LOYALTY THROUGH MOMENTS THAT MATTER
- Birthdays
- Special Holidays
- Work anniversary
- Pregnancy and birth; return to work
- Bereavement
- Medical Leave

MOVEMENTS: GROWTH AND DEVELOPMENT
- Learning & Development continuous journey
- Career Development, Coaching & Mentorship
- Talent Management conversations
- Personal Development Plans
- Cross-training and Cross Exposure to different departments
- Internal Mobility Programs: promotions, lateral moves, secondments
- Moving entities/subsidiaries (cross-boarding)

CULTURE & ENGAGEMENT
- Ongoing culture acclimatization and training
- Ongoing Engagement Surveys
- Ongoing Rewards, Recognition & Celebration
- Mental Health and Wellbeing Agenda
- Brand Advocacy
- Events, Activities & Networking
- Company Asset Tours (if applicable)

STEP 4: OFFBOARDING AND REBOARDING

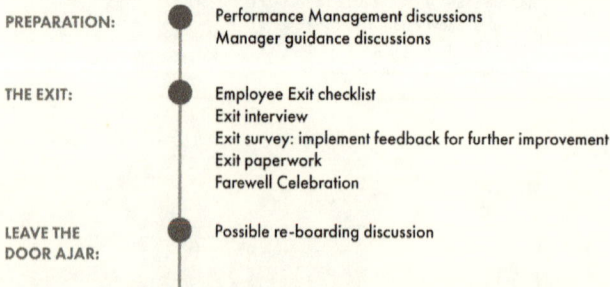

PREPARATION:
- Performance Management discussions
- Manager guidance discussions

THE EXIT:
- Employee Exit checklist
- Exit interview
- Exit survey: implement feedback for further improvement
- Exit paperwork
- Farewell Celebration

LEAVE THE DOOR AJAR:
- Possible re-boarding discussion

FIGURE 4. THE EMPLOYEE JOURNEY ROADMAP

It's important to note that the touchpoints related to engaging, growing, and performing are not linear and are not one-time occurrences. They happen multiple times at any point throughout the journey. The content of the roadmap aims to serve as an inspiration and a guideline to tailor your company employee journey.

As promised at the beginning of the chapter, we have covered the first three touchpoints that a new joiner should experience. The employer brand and the company's external reputation play a significant role in attracting the right talent. How they are treated throughout the interview cycle and the pre-boarding stage can influence whether they join the company or not. At this point, the hiring manager's involvement is crucial because people join companies but leave managers. So, a genuine relationship based on mutual respect between the employee and the manager is one of the cornerstones of an incredible employee journey.

The next section of this book focuses on the engaging, developing, and performing stages of the employee journey. If supported correctly, these stages elicit employee productivity, loyalty, and a genuine sense of workplace happiness. These will automatically translate to a great employee experience and a memorable customer experience. I'm excited to share the next section with you. Let's dive in!

CHALLENGE ACCEPTED: PUTTING *ATTRACTING, IDENTIFYING, HIRING, ONBOARDING* INTO ACTION

Have some fun when engaging in the following suggested activities. These activities directly apply this chapter's concepts and will help you translate its insights into tangible actions for creating a more positive and engaging employee experience in your organization.

1. Personal Vision Board Workshop

Task: Guide employees through creating individual vision boards that visually represent their ideal employee experience, incorporating elements like desired roles, skills, recognition, and workplace environment.

Challenge: Encourage participants to use images, quotes, and affirmations that resonate with their personal aspirations.

Activity: Share and discuss vision boards in small groups, fostering understanding and empathy for each other's desired experiences. Encourage employees to keep their vision boards visible as a reminder of their goals and motivators for ongoing engagement.

2. Fearless Feedback Festival

Task: Organize a dedicated quarterly activity where new employees feel empowered to share constructive feedback on company policies, processes, and culture. Use anonymous surveys, suggestion boxes, or open-forum discussions.

Challenge: Ensure a safe and respectful environment where their voices are heard and valued. Frame feedback as an opportunity for continuous improvement and positive change.

Activity: Collect and prioritize feedback, acknowledging contributors and developing concrete action plans to address the most common concerns about their current employee experience.

3. Spark Your 'Iron Lady' (or Iron Man) Spirit

Task: Identify a personal or professional goal that ignites your passion and determination, similar to my desire to become a flight attendant with Emirates Airlines.

Challenge: Break down your goal into smaller, achievable steps and create a concrete action plan to move forward.

Activity: Schedule weekly/monthly 'Iron Lady' check-ins to track your progress, celebrate milestones, and adjust your plan as needed. Channel the little girl's (or boy's) unwavering spirit to overcome obstacles and persevere in pursuit of your dreams.

PART 3 Creating Moments that Matter

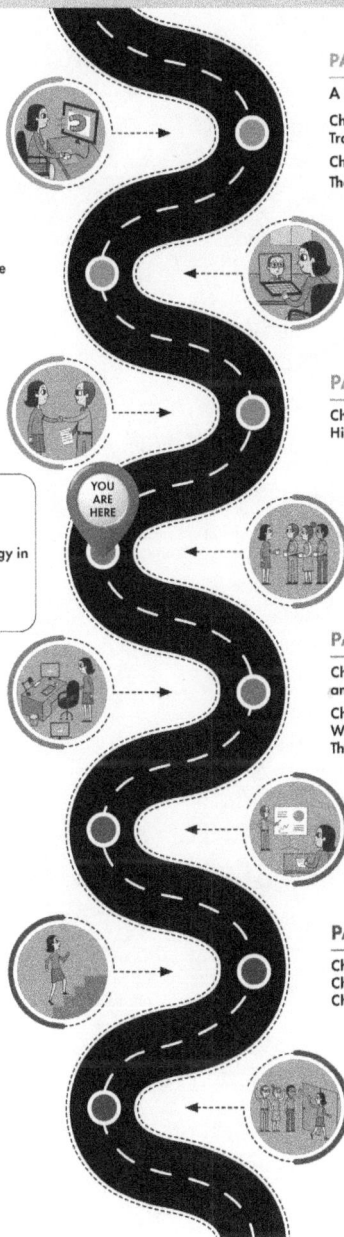

CHAPTER 7

ENGAGE

"Research indicates that workers have three prime needs: interesting work, recognition for a good job, and being let in on things that are going on in the company."

—ZIG ZIGLAR

Some of you may disagree with this quotation. However, work means different things to different people, and everyone engages with and commits to work differently. Sometimes, leaders think that excellent remuneration and salary increments drive employee engagement. Money may drive employee satisfaction, but it does not play a primary and exclusive role in holistic, long-term engagement. In this chapter, I define employee engagement according to various sources. I will discuss the difference between employee satisfaction, happiness, and engagement. I will also discuss the psychology behind employee engagement, what a meaningful workplace is, and how this can be created. By the end of this chapter, you will understand what drives employee engagement and how you can apply it to your workplaces.

SOME DEFINITIONS OF EMPLOYEE ENGAGEMENT

It's essential to understand that employee engagement, satisfaction, and happiness are all different. An employee can be satisfied with a job without being engaged. Someone could be happy at work because they get to see their best friends, or perhaps working with robotics to deliver life-saving packages to dangerous geographical zones is a source of happiness and fulfillment for individuals. One could be unsatisfied because their salary isn't high enough to cover expenses, or they might be disengaged because their boss has passed over them for several promotions. Employee happiness and employee satisfaction lead to employee engagement, which in turn has a positive effect on the overall employee experience. As such, employee satisfaction is one of the components of employee engagement, and employee engagement is one of the components of the employee experience.

Professor John Purcell, a people-management expert, defines employee engagement as "a combination of attitude and behavior." The attitude is "commitment" and the behavior is "going the extra mile." Another renowned definition stems from the 2009 MacLeod Report, in which the authors suggest that engagement is possible if the workplace and culture craft and maintain an environment for individuals to thrive. According to the report, employee engagement benefits both the employee and the employer and is defined as:

"A workplace approach designed to ensure that employees are committed to their organization's goals and values, motivated to contribute to organizational success, and are able at the same time to enhance their own sense of wellbeing."

We often discuss why employee engagement is essential for an organization, but we rarely mention the benefits of employee engagement for the actual employees. A major advantage is an improvement in overall wellbeing.

Although William Kahn is considered the father of employee engagement, the most widely used definition in the literature is from Schaufeli and colleagues (2002). Their model of engagement stems from burnout literature. According to them, burnout is a lasting state of disengagement in which employees experience emotional exhaustion, depersonalization, and decreased personal accomplishment. These authors, therefore, proposed that engagement is the opposite of burnout. They defined employee engagement as having three components: rigor, dedication, and absorption. Rigor refers to the energy expended at work and the persistence to continue one's work. Dedication is involvement in one's work with pride and enthusiasm. Absorption entails total concentration or being in the state of flow. Flow is further discussed in the chapter on wellbeing.

The concept of employee engagement involves understanding constructs such as happiness, satisfaction, motivation, burnout, meaningfulness, availability, job identification, and citizenship behaviors (the willingness for employees to go above and beyond their role). Kahn relied on Jackman and Oldham's Job Characteristics Theory (JCT) from 1980 to develop his framework. Besides interpersonal relations and needs satisfaction, the so-called 'contextual job factors' are also essential to review. The JCT model proposes specific characteristics of the workplace that lead to motivation and impact behavioral outcomes. These dimensions, which should be considered from as early as selecting and hiring, are:

- skill variety (the need to use multiple skills in one's job)
- task significance (the value of the task to the organizational goal)

- task identity (how individuals identify internally with their tasks)
- autonomy (having empowerment and control over one's work, plans, and goals)
- feedback (must be constructive, objective, and timely).

THE PSYCHOLOGY BEHIND EMPLOYEE ENGAGEMENT

Research going back as far as the 1920s—namely the famous Hawthorne Studies, which focused on organizational behavior—provided the cornerstones for future studies on the influences and drivers of human productivity. This research suggested that focusing on what is wrong in an organization and dealing with it may prevent employee dissatisfaction, but it did not necessarily lead to positive outcomes, higher employee engagement, and better performance. Instead, psychologists Luthans and Youssef said that a positive approach to managing human resources was needed to witness positive attitudes and outstanding business outcomes.

Once you attract, hire, and onboard your employees, the fourth step in the employee lifecycle is to continuously engage them. Employee engagement has tremendous influence over the employee experience. This chapter will delineate what leaders must focus on to make employee engagement work for them and their colleagues. What is it exactly, and why is it important?

Employee engagement is the extent to which employees find value, meaning, and purpose in what they do and the extent to which they choose to invest their physical, emotional, and mental energy into making their organization a success. In fact, there are various types of employee engagement. According to Dr. Shoobridge, a renowned leader on this subject, these are:

- rational engagement—employees understand and support the organization's values
- emotional engagement—employees are proud to work in the organization
- motivational engagement—employees are willing to go above and beyond at work
- devotional engagement—employees are loyal to the organization.

This matters to an organization because a consistently high employee engagement rate is linked to innovation, connection, collaboration, communication between employees, talent attraction and retention, and reduced employee turnover. It also brings tremendous business results.

In 1990, William Kahn proposed that group dynamics, supervisory styles, worker participation, growth and development, self-actualization, and increased attention were major contributors to positive attitudes and performance.

Further research posits that employee engagement refers to the motivational state of an employee and holds that employees offer different degrees and dimensions of themselves at work according to both conscious and unconscious feelings. Engagement at work requires employees to feel a connection between their work and their personal meanings and purposes in life. Engagement is recognized when people put in discretionary effort, remain focused, and are completely involved with and committed to what they do. Kahn further proposes that engaged employees are physically and psychologically present at work, demonstrated when they are attentive, connected, integrated, and absorbed.

Workplaces can shape the extent to which employees feel engaged by fostering the necessary conditions for engagement to thrive. Research by Macey and Schneider (2008) demonstrated that engagement is not static, and an employee's experience of the workplace at different moments in time can cause fluctuations in engagement. Thus, employers must create environments where engagement can consistently flourish. According to Kahn, the following are necessary conditions for this to happen:

- Meaningfulness—does the employee find their work meaningful enough to bring and engage their whole self?
- Safety/psychological safety—does the employee feel safe expressing themselves without negative consequences?
- Availability—is the employee mentally and physically available to bring themselves to work?

Engagement may vary on a regular basis, so let's keep in mind that sometimes the answers to these questions can vary depending on when they are asked. For example, some work tasks may be more meaningful, or perhaps a particular group of individuals may be more supportive of the employee than others. These everyday factors influence the above-mentioned conditions.

Other researchers in employee engagement confirm that people derive meaning from work when they know their voices matter and if they have meaningful relationships with those around them. Work matters more to people if they feel connected to others. Work is more meaningful when employees do things together, have fun, and learn about themselves and each other. This is one reason why employee engagement and wellbeing rates plummeted in 2020. The global COVID-19 pandemic created mass isolation, and people's connections to their workplaces and workmates were shaken to the core.

WORKPLACE MEANINGFULNESS

According to Steger, a prominent figure in the study of meaning, being able to derive meaning from our environment is paramount to wellbeing. The ability to find understanding and significance in work is a substantial motivating factor. It allows employees to achieve a sense of worth through their daily actions and indicates what more they should be doing to have a better quality of life. Studies suggest that people who believe their lives have meaning and purpose are happier, can enjoy greater wellbeing, are more satisfied with life, have greater control over their lives, and are more engaged with their work. Individuals with a greater sense of meaning are also more positive overall.

How do we get more meaning from life? World-renowned psychologist Wong describes seven sources of meaning:

- relationships
- intimacy
- self-transcendence
- achievement
- self-acceptance
- fairness/respect
- spirituality.

Emmons adds one more source from which we derive meaning: work.

According to Steger, meaningful work matters because it is associated with greater wellbeing, employee engagement, and reduced employee turnover. Steger also suggests that people who say their work is meaningful demonstrate better psychological adjustment and qualities that are desirable to organizations.

Many people look for meaningful work because they derive fulfillment from it. One way to do this is by identifying what type of role would align with your values, desires, beliefs, and motives. The word 'authentic' is derived from the Greek word *authenteo*, which means 'to have full power'. In humanistic psychology, authenticity is a central construct and necessary for wellbeing.

How are meaningful work experiences cultivated for employees? And what are the potential individual and organizational benefits experienced when people are oriented to experience meaningfulness at work?

HOW AND WHY IS MEANINGFULNESS FOSTERED AT WORK?

Meaningfulness at work is both self-constructed and socially constructed. This means we can build it personally, and/or society can help construct or shape it. In Pratt and Ashforth's research on linking positive organizational psychology with fostering meaningfulness at work, the authors propose that individuals construct their own meaning according to their identities, and that for companies to foster meaning for their employees (which leads to engagement), they must influence how people regard themselves. However, what is meaningful to one person may not be to another.

A person's work orientation has a lot to do with this. Work orientation refers to someone's opinion about what makes the job worth doing: Is it a job, a career, or a calling? This is externally influenced by sources such as friends, colleagues, family, the rest of society, and media. It can change over time according to a person's marital status, spirituality, and education. According to Bellah and colleagues, a person who views work as a job looks at it as something that provides financial security, whilst someone who looks at it as a career can derive meaning through success, promotions, and recognition. Calling, as a work orientation, provides someone with meaning and value. A calling connects a person to their colleagues and to a larger community. This is discussed in more detail in the chapter on rewards and recognition.

For my Master of Science in Applied Positive Psychology, my final dissertation project explored how teaching individuals about their personal wellbeing through meaningful gamification and experiential learning fostered quality bonds. I envisaged and designed an escape room to teach players about wellbeing. My design featured a series of rooms with puzzles, quizzes, and activities that helped to focus the participants' attention on Buckinghamshire's five ways to wellbeing:

- be active
- keep learning
- take notice
- connect
- give.

In addition, I focused my research and writing on creating a sense of connectedness, employee engagement, mindfulness, gratitude, and personal transformations. Earlier, I spoke about memorable and transformational customer and employee experiences. By encouraging employees to focus on their wellbeing, organizations also help them find meaning in their jobs. This is, of course, beneficial for the business and the wider community. However, this may not be the case with employees for whom work is merely a job, not a career or a calling. So, what else can organizations do to go beyond employee engagement?

Contrary to popular belief, employee engagement is not simply fun and games! The science and numbers behind the benefits of employee engagement prove that it is an essential part of any thriving industry and business. According to Kincentric's employee engagement model, *Say Stay Strive*, engaged employees **say** great things about their organization, happily **stay** and work in that organization, and **strive** to do their best and go above and beyond the call of duty. This means organizations with high employee engagement levels have good employer branding and employee advocacy, which helps attract and retain top talent. Because employee turnover is low, they also don't spend excessive money on hiring every year, which saves money to be used for various employee benefits. And lastly, employees that strive will undoubtedly create great customer experiences and increase customer and brand loyalty.

So far, we have discussed various dimensions to consider when deploying an employee engagement strategy. I will conclude this chapter by considering the enablers of employee engagement.

ENABLERS OF EMPLOYEE ENGAGEMENT

There is a great deal of academic work on what drives engagement. Throughout this book, I share knowledge I have gathered through my experience as an employee and as a consultant while interacting with senior leaders, team members, and other consultants. This is my signature authentic, holistic, and long-lasting employee engagement model.

FIGURE 5. ENABLERS OF EMPLOYEE ENGAGEMENT

1. **Enabler: Positive Workplaces**
   Goal: Use positive psychology to create a positive and thriving work environment through constructs such as wellbeing, gratitude, appreciation, love, joy, hope, resilience, goal setting, and strengths spotting. Apply positive psychology to develop policies, training modules, leadership facilitation, and goal setting.

2. **Enabler: Internal Communication**
   Goal: Communicate with clarity, compassion, purpose, and anticipation, ensuring that you have your audience in mind. Be sure to enable three-way communication (top to bottom, bottom-up, and sideways), and remember the "who, what, when, where, why, how many, how much" when adopting a mixed-media communication approach.

3. **Enabler: Rewards, Recognition, Motivation, Pride, Celebration, and Remuneration and Benefits**
   Goal: Engage colleagues and celebrate their achievements through various meaningful and timely rewards and recognition ceremonies, encouraging them to strive for excellence. Ensure your remuneration and benefits package is competitive to attract and retain the right people and help them feel valued and appreciated.

4. **Enabler: Wellbeing**
   Goal: Foster a learning climate and culture through building an inclusive employee wellbeing strategy where people can connect through elements of social, physical, mental, financial, nutritional, and communal wellbeing; an environment where teamwork and camaraderie are valued and essential, and peer-to-peer relationships and loyalty are considered vital to overall success.

5. **Enabler: Organizational Values and Goals**

   Goal: Promote organizational values that instill a sense of commitment and pride—values that are purposeful and drive a culture aligned with diversity, equity, equality, inclusion, belonging, and mattering. With the support of the organizational values, create meaningful goals based on innovation and continuous improvement and ensure that people feel connected to them. Show people how they fit into the overall business strategy and how they make a difference.

6. **Enabler: Engaging and Approachable Leadership**

   Goal: Hire and train leaders that will instill and demonstrate care, involvement, equity, transparency, and visibility amongst all colleagues—leaders that are respectful, sincere, trustworthy, and who walk the talk. Develop leaders that are loved by their teams and whose presence and contribution encourage employee retention. People join companies but leave managers.

7. **Enabler: Growth, Development, and Retention**

   Goal: Nurture an environment and culture where colleagues fully understand their roles and want to stay and work with you. A workplace must not encourage stagnation and should enable people to continuously grow and advance in their careers through succession planning, promotions (vertical/horizontal), changes in responsibilities, and improved skills, capabilities, and knowledge.

8. **Enabler: Culture and Change Management**

   Goal: Create a workplace that considers the physical, technological, and cultural environments—an organization that employees feel part of and where any changes to the culture are done *with* them, not *to* them. Ensure that employees are excited and feel actively involved in shaping their own future at work.

9. **Enabler: Employee Advocacy**

   Goal: Give employees a voice. They are the biggest brand ambassadors, and if they genuinely love and actively promote the company, customers will do the same.

10. **Result: Employee Experience**

    Goal: Map out the entire employee experience journey from when people are attracted to your employer brand to when they exit your company as alumni, and make that experience employee-centric. Remember all the touchpoints and moments that matter to every organizational persona and align them to your culture through continuous colleague feedback.

Bear in mind that every organization and its culture is different. Accordingly, leaders must concentrate on some engagement enablers more than others. For instance, organizations in their early stages will require much more work on creating and embedding their culture, mission, purpose, vision, core values, and behaviors. Other organizations may be going through change management, which requires different combinations of enablers, such as increased internal communication, employee advocacy, and leadership visibility. A more mature organization might be gearing up for expansion or acquiring another company and may concentrate its engagement efforts on developing and growing its middle managers to be ready for future promotions.

These enablers will be instrumental in creating a successful and authentic employee engagement strategy. The HR and leadership team should concentrate their efforts on establishing a culture-centric employee experience based on feedback from colleagues and a motivation strategy that draws inspiration from engagement facilitators. For this to happen, understanding their teams is crucial and can be done by cultivating meaningful connections and deeply understanding what drives individual employees.

Engagement increases if the organization puts their intentions in the right places. But for this to happen, it is essential for engagement levels to be measured on a regular interval—at least twice a year. In Chapter 14, I address qualitative and quantitative metrics on measuring engagement. I also look at how this integrates with other company metrics telling the complete story behind the customer and the employee experience.

WHAT DO WE KNOW SO FAR?

This chapter discussed the origins of employee engagement and reviewed various definitions, keeping in mind that happiness and satisfaction are critical components of employee engagement, and engagement is a crucial component of an excellent employee experience. We also looked at how to foster workplace meaningfulness. Lastly, I presented my signature model of enablers of employee engagement and proposed ways you can implement these enablers at work. I will continue to unveil concrete guidance on implementing the enablers in the coming chapters.

As we enter this complex segment of the employee lifecycle, we must acknowledge that everyone is accountable for delivering employee engagement. Let's embrace this responsibility and take ownership. Engagement primarily comes from the top down, and leadership tremendously influences engagement, disengagement, motivation, and demotivation. However, we must remember that, as human beings, we are ultimately responsible for our own engagement, just like we are for our motivation, happiness, or potential burnout! We cannot sit back and relax, relying solely on the goodness and leadership of others to create meaningful workplaces for us, to take care of our growth and performance, and to reward and recognize us when we perform well. Similarly, we cannot demand and expect workplaces to always get it right. We all have a role to play. This is why the first step employees must take is to know themselves, their values, what drives and demotivates them, and their personal and professional goals. In turn, leaders and HR departments are responsible for creating and fostering an environment where colleagues thrive and flourish.

This brings me to the next topic: the adoption of positive psychology at work and how this can significantly shape employee engagement, the employee experience, and the customer experience. Employee engagement and the science of positive psychology go hand in hand. In the workplace, we can use positive psychology interventions to implement an employee engagement strategy that is meaningful and science-based, not just a collection of random ad hoc happiness-boosting events. Please join me in exploring positive psychology and how this science affects organizational behavior.

CHALLENGE ACCEPTED: PUTTING *EMPLOYEE ENGAGEMENT* INTO ACTION

And here are this chapter's recommended activities. They are designed to promote collaboration, shared purpose, and team-based growth. By doing these activities, I hope to encourage you to move beyond individual engagement and create a truly connected and thriving work environment for everyone.

1. Monthly Random Acts of Teamwork

Task: Encourage team members to perform small, unexpected acts of kindness and support for each other. This could involve offering help with tasks, celebrating personal achievements, or expressing appreciation for someone's contribution.

Challenge: Focus on genuine gestures that come from the heart.

Activity: Track and share these Random Acts of Teamwork on a dedicated platform. This creates a positive ripple effect, fostering stronger bonds and a more supportive team environment.

2. Engagement Audit by Peers

Task: Design a peer-to-peer engagement audit process for each department where employees anonymously provide feedback on team dynamics, collaboration, and individual contributions.

Challenge: Shift the focus from individual performance to building a supportive team environment. Focus on identifying areas for improvement together.

Activity: Facilitate group discussions based on the anonymized audit results. Work together to develop action plans to enhance team engagement. This empowers employees to take ownership of their work environment and build a more positive and engaging team culture.

3. Engagement Metric Dashboard

Task: Design a custom dashboard featuring key metrics related to engagement, such as employee turnover, absenteeism, customer feedback, and survey results.

Challenge: Track these metrics over time and identify trends to improve your engagement strategy.

Activity: Regularly review the dashboard with leadership. Discuss correlations, celebrate successes, and use data to foster continuous improvement.

CHAPTER 8

POSITIVE PSYCHOLOGY IN ORGANIZATIONS

In a constantly evolving society, work modes change quickly and organizations that are not sufficiently agile are regularly forced out of business. Experts predict that 50% of today's occupations will no longer be relevant in the coming couple of years. In an increasingly volatile, uncertain, complex, and ambiguous environment (VUCA), leaders constantly evaluate different approaches to staying in business. Due to workplace and societal changes, individuals are becoming increasingly disengaged at work and are looking for ways to derive greater self-actualization. Longer working hours, work intensification, burnout, ineffective leadership, and downsizing have increased employee cynicism and mistrust—even more so since the onset of the COVID-19 pandemic and the wave of the Great Resignation and quiet quitting.

In the last two and a half decades, businesses have turned to evidence-based approaches that create resilient teams, enhance achievement, and improve creativity, innovation, and wellbeing. In this chapter, we will review the science of positive psychology, examine positive workplaces and relationships, and determine how to create and sustain them. I will discuss practical examples of how positive psychology can be applied at work to increase positive organizational behavior, employee engagement, and wellbeing. By the end of this chapter, you should appreciate that leaders and organizations who adopt positive psychology will enjoy flourishing and inspirational workplaces and be able to create positive influences through their actions. Proactively integrating the science of positive psychology into your employee experience strategy will help increase positive customer experiences.

MY FIRST EXPERIENCE WITH POSITIVE PSYCHOLOGY

In 2017, I had the pleasure of speaking at a happiness event. My keynote focused on personal and workplace happiness. Two of my co-presenters were Lesley Lyle and Dan Collinson, lecturers in applied positive psychology at Buckinghamshire New University in the UK. Until then, I had a vague understanding of positive psychology and was extremely excited after listening to their keynote on happiness. After getting to know them and their work better, I was convinced I had to study for a Master of Science in Applied Positive Psychology at their university. And what a wonderful experience that was! I have always been interested in positive psychology constructs such as self-transformation, resilience, strengths spotting, gratitude, and emotions. I wanted to contribute even more meaningfully at work by applying this science to employee engagement.

During my studies, I attended a summit on positive psychology in Bedford, UK, where I met Sarah Lewis, a scholar, author, and speaker with a wealth of knowledge on the topic. Her motivating keynote and outstanding book, *Positive Psychology at Work*, have heavily influenced how I work and are a major inspiration for this chapter. The strategies for employee engagement and employee experience that I have implemented were heavily influenced by the science of positive psychology and organizational psychology. This has resulted in significantly increased employee engagement and guest satisfaction scores. This chapter will give you an overview of how you can adopt positive psychology to create positive workplaces, along with some practical examples that you can implement.

Enjoy the ride!

POSITIVE PSYCHOLOGY AND POSITIVE THINKING ARE NOT THE SAME

Let's begin with a quick distinction between positive thinking and positive psychology. These two terms are often confused.

Positive psychology is the science of wellbeing. It studies what is *right* with people and differs from traditional psychology, which focuses on what is *wrong* with people. It focuses on creating flourishing states for humans and cultivating growth by going beyond fixing what is 'not right.'

Positive psychology is the academic study of what makes life worth living and what allows people and communities to thrive. It also studies the conditions for optimal functioning amongst individuals, teams, and work.

Positive psychology is subject to scientific experimentation and research; it is reliable and repeatable. It has a body of knowledge—academic courses, colleges, universities, departments, and professors. It is about helping people live a good, happy, and productive life. The study of positive psychology also includes negative emotions (the dark side of positive psychology) and their importance to our wellbeing. Emotions such as stress, fear, sadness, anxiety, and anger are necessary because they highlight potential threats to our wellbeing and urge us to escape that danger.

On the other hand, positive thinking deals with the power of influencing things via your way of thinking (i.e., attracting good things with positive thoughts and attracting bad things with negative thoughts).

Positive psychology as a science proposes ways to help individuals develop their ability to cultivate particular psychological states—such as optimism, flow, and resilience—which help them at work and in their everyday lives.

WHAT IS A POSITIVE WORKPLACE?
From Human Capital to Positive Psychological Capital (and in Between)

In the late 1990s, the father of positive psychology, Martin Seligman, suggested that the construct of positive psychology consists of three areas: positive emotions, positive traits, and positive institutions (or workplaces) where people flourish.

Figure 6, taken from Luthans et al. (2004), demonstrates the evolution of employees to the biggest asset a company can have. Historically, the key to achieving business success has been having adequate economic capital. It was all about 'what you have.' Today, an increasing number of individuals believe that having highly skilled and motivated employees is key to gaining a competitive edge in business. It's about 'what you know.' Influential leaders recognize this. Aligning human capital with corporate strategy has a notable positive effect on performance outcomes. Fully engaged and committed employees make a substantial positive difference.

In the following figure, the third column pertains to social capital. This concept involves facilitating appropriate resources, high-quality relationships, effective networking, and trust. It is all about 'who you know' instead of 'what you know.' The interactions that occur within an organization have a significant impact on its overall capability.

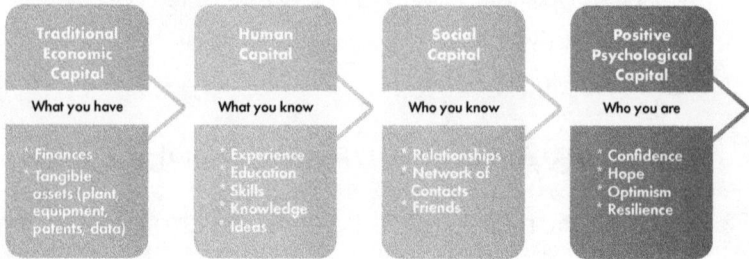

Traditional Economic Capital	Human Capital	Social Capital	Positive Psychological Capital
What you have	What you know	Who you know	Who you are
* Finances * Tangible assets (plant, equipment, patents, data)	* Experience * Education * Skills * Knowledge * Ideas	* Relationships * Network of Contacts * Friends	* Confidence * Hope * Optimism * Resilience

FIGURE 6. EXPANDING CAPITAL FOR COMPETITIVE ADVANTAGE

Investing in social capital is important for organizations' success and competitive advantage. It is also essential for building trust, effective communication, and collaboration. The fourth column discusses the positive psychological capital related to employee development. Scholars propose adopting positive psychological capital in workplaces to help organizations unleash their potential for doing good through specific initiatives.

According to psychologists Luthans and Youssef, on a macro level, the construct of positive-oriented initiatives in the workplace is referred to as positive organizational scholarship (POS). POS integrates positive psychology and organizational research. It is concerned with positive outcomes and, according to Cameron (2003), focuses on the dynamics of excellence, flourishing, thriving, virtuousness, and abundance.

On a micro level, positive organizational behavior (POB) is considered a driver of the development and performance of human resources. The domain of POB includes positive psychology constructs such as self-efficacy (confidence), hope, optimism, and resilience. These four elements combined are known as psychological capital, or PsyCap, and they can be developed through specific employee activities to demonstrate high-performance impact.

Luthans and colleagues (2007) defined PsyCap as follows:

"An individual's positive psychological state of development that is characterized by: 1) having confidence (self-efficacy) to take on and put in the necessary effort to succeed at challenging tasks; 2) making a positive attribution (optimism) about succeeding now and in the future; 3) preserving towards goals and, when necessary, redirecting paths to goals (hope) in order to succeed; and 4) when beset by problems and adversity, sustaining and bouncing back and even beyond (resilience) to attain success."

POS was developed to enhance organizations' performance and bring out the extraordinary in them through positive practices and the positive behavior of their employees. A vast body of evidence discusses the advantages of applying positive psychology at work and its effect on enhanced engagement, collaboration, innovation, wellbeing, and productivity (Green, Evans, & Williams, 2017). Organizations and their teams can demonstrate extraordinary performance by understanding the drivers of positive work practices.

Several relevant and actionable theories lead to POS. These are the broaden and build theory (Fredrickson 1998), hope theory (Snyder, 2000), self-determination theory (SDT) (Deci & Ryan 1985, 1991), and the positive emotion, engagement, relationships, meaning, and accomplishment model (PERMA; Seligman, 2011), as well as the self-efficacy (Bandura, 1997), optimism (Schneider, 2001), and resilience (Masten, 2001) theories. The practical application of these theories correlates with positive outcomes for organizations and employees, such as improved wellbeing, optimal performance, better business results, and growth. Throughout this chapter, I will discuss some of these theories. A detailed account is, however, outside of the scope of this book, and I suggest that you engage in further research if you're interested in more details. I've included some excellent resources in the reference section at the end of this book. For now, let's take a further look at positive workplaces.

According to Cameron (2009), three things make up a workplace culture where positivity, abundance, connectivity, and optimism thrive:

1. Focusing on **positive deviance**: Organizations with positive deviance regularly thrive and generally contribute to the wellbeing of their colleagues, customers, and society. They aim high, focus on growing excellence, and encourage extraordinary performance instead of preventing bad things from happening. They also focus on their teams' and individual members' strengths through strengths-spotting and strengths-building exercises. Building on someone's strengths, rather than focusing on and improving on their weaknesses, is a pervasive and highly effective use of positive psychology in the workplace.

2. Demonstrating **virtuous actions**: Actions such as trust, generosity, forgiveness, optimism, compassion, and integrity encourage others to pay it forward. This is associated with enhanced teamwork, positive emotions, employee commitment, and

social capital. In Buckinghamshire's five ways to wellbeing, two of those ways are 'giving' (being generous) and 'taking notice' (being mindful); these are virtuous actions. Research by Cameron and colleagues shows that a business that develops an organizational climate with high levels of virtuousness positively correlates with performance (customer loyalty, innovation, revenue, innovation, and quality).

3. Cultivating **affirmative bias**: This means focusing on the best rather than the worst to grow by analyzing and utilizing organizational strengths and capabilities, not weaknesses and problems, to communicate and to develop relationships. As Lewis says, strategic development becomes a vibrant and engaging process that produces positive change. As an alternative to the commonly used SWOT (strengths, weaknesses, opportunities, and threats) analysis, Stavros, Cooperrider, and Kelley (2003) proposed a SOAR (strengths, opportunities, aspirations, and results) model. I love this model because its direction is based on appreciative inquiry principles, which I will discuss further below. The questions participants should be asked are:

- What are our greatest assets?
- What are the best possible market opportunities?
- What is the preferred future?
- What are the measurable results?

During hard times or trauma, such as that brought about by the COVID-19 pandemic, for instance, an organization abundant in positive relationships is more resilient and robust than an organization where trust and camaraderie are scarce.

I wonder what type of workplace culture you are cultivating. What are you doing to promote positive deviance and affirmative bias? Is your organization known for performing virtuous actions internally for colleagues and externally for customers and the community? The actions of employees affect the organization's performance.

The next section will review how to use positive psychology to create a thriving workplace.

HOW TO CREATE POSITIVE WORKPLACES

There is an abundance of practical literature on how people can use positive psychology to create positive workplaces. You may know some of the ways and already be using them. Let's briefly review my highly recommended ones.

Building psychological capital at work is essential, so I share a model from Lewis (2011), influenced by what Luthans and colleagues suggested in 2007. This will help leaders develop PsyCap in their workplaces.

1. Developing self-efficacy:
    - Provide learning and growth opportunities and avoid throwing employees in the deep end unless you know they will persevere and succeed.
    - Provide good mentorship and coaching programs.
    - Be an encouraging leader and help instill in colleagues the confidence and trust that they will succeed.
    - Ensure that people look after themselves.

---

2. Encouraging hope:
   - Use goal setting effectively and involve individuals in setting their goals.
   - Positively reinforce hopeful behavior.
   - Use an involving, participatory, and empowering leadership style, such as appropriate and genuine delegation, group decision-making, and colleagues' involvement, in building the workplace culture.
3. Developing optimism:
   - Counteract pessimism by encouraging self-forgiveness and helping people spot and grab opportunities.
4. Developing resilience:
   - Help people learn from setbacks so that they can experience post-traumatic growth.
   - Help develop mindfulness and encourage individuals to be more aware of how their physical and mental states affect their resilience.

Appreciative inquiry is an inquiry into some aspect of organizational life, and it is appreciative in nature, focusing on the best of the present and the past. It is a positive strengths-based change methodology that can be used on individuals, organizations, and society to help identify and understand the reasons for their success. This method of inquiry proposes that instead of working to eliminate what we do not want, we concentrate and augment more of what we do want. It can be used in organizations to build upon the strength of the workforce.

The principle of appreciative inquiry was developed in 1987 by Cooperrider and Srivastva, and it is crucial for releasing the positive potential of people, creating positive emotions and positive change as a result. Appreciative inquiry is based on four processes:

- discovering the best of the present
- co-creating attractive futures
- redesigning an organization
- working together to make things happen.

It is built around the 4D model of intervention: discovery, dream, design, and destiny.

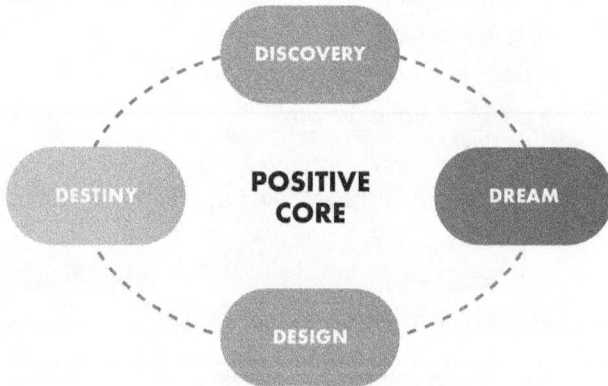

Appreciative Inquiry 4-D Process

FIGURE 7. APPRECIATIVE INQUIRY 4D PROCESS

How can this be achieved in the workplace? Through appreciative inquiry's questioning process, individuals are asked about achievements, good times, and success. By asking about happy moments, the interviewer intensifies moments of pride, wellbeing, and positive emotions. Practitioners of appreciative inquiry ask questions that evoke positive emotions in people, creating the possibility of visualizing and thus building a better future for them. This method can also be used during recruitment interviews.

If you are wondering about the script of appreciative inquiry and how to conduct a positive line of questioning, Lewis proposes the following three types of questions that encourage the responder to think about the past, present, and future:

1. Tell me about a time when you completed a project within your deadlines and to an exceptionally high quality.
   - What happened?
   - How did you do this?
   - What did others do to help?
   - What other factors were present that helped this happen?
   - What did you do particularly well?
   - What made that situation special so that it stands out from the rest?
2. What do you value about the way the team works currently? What must we keep doing?
3. Thinking about the future, you have three wishes:
   - What do you want more of?
   - What do you want less of?
   - What do you think we could be doing differently?

POSITIVE EMOTIONS

What I appreciate about positive emotions is that they are a source of energy for change. The scientist most credited with the study of positive emotion is Barbara Fredrickson, who, in 1998, introduced the broaden-and-build theory of positive emotions, which proposes that positive emotions such as hope, interest, gratitude, and joy *broaden* peoples' thought–action repertoires and *build* resources that are critical for wellbeing. According to Fredrickson and Losada, positive emotions are the most essential ingredient for human flourishing.

As proposed by Isen and Fredrickson in 2005 and adapted by Lewis in her book *Positive Psychology at Work*, here are some scientifically proven ways organizations can benefit from encouraging and enabling their teams to experience positive emotions at work. Feeling good undoes the harmful effects of feeling bad. People experiencing positive emotions such as joy, passion, pride, and optimism:

- are more creative
- show improved negotiation processes and outcomes
- are more thorough in what they do
- are more open-minded
- display more flexible thinking/problem-solving
- show more generosity
- are more motivated to achieve their goals
- can think more clearly and handle complex information
- are likely to have a reduced amount of interpersonal conflict.

There is considerable research in organizational psychology on the link between positive individual behavior (employee retention and work engagement) and a positive culture, which leads to organizational outcomes such as profitability, customer relationships, and reduced employee turnover.

Positive and engaging leadership: Good leadership can be expressed through various leadership styles, such as servant, charismatic, transformative, visionary, directive, and participatory. Positivity is strongly associated with authentic leadership. Leaders who are authentic exhibit positive behaviors, inspire commitment, and demonstrate their belief that everyone on the team is valuable. Avolio and colleagues (2010) discovered four key facets to authentic leadership.

1. **Relational transparency**: being transparent in your relationships and not pretending.
2. **Internal morality**: having an internal reference point of what is morally right or wrong.
3. **Adaptive self-reflection**: being mindful and capable of reflecting on your own behavior with as little bias as possible and learning from certain situations that have arisen.
4. **Balanced processing**: objectively analyzing all relevant information before reaching a conclusion.

Avolio and colleagues also found that authentic leaders create authentic followers who emulate the qualities their leaders display. This means they can generate a highly engaged, positive, and ethical organizational culture.

Positive communication is when authentic and genuine positive language replaces negative and critical language. Positive comments foster positive feelings, and positive feelings enhance connectivity. Negative comments should also be mindfully communicated, not ignored. Feedback must be given in a corrective, supportive, and constructive way. One must be mindful of focusing on strengths rather than weaknesses, as well as on the language and sentence construction used. Positive communication yields positive results, and constructive feedback strengthens relationships (if done correctly).

Best self-feedback: Developed by Cameron (2008), this approach is the opposite of the typical 360-degree feedback that organizations often implement. The best self-feedback survey template encourages fifteen to twenty respondents to assess and recount three short instances where the individual has made a positive workplace contribution or has represented themselves in the best possible light. Sample questions include:

When you have seen me make a special or valuable contribution, what distinctive strengths did I display?

When you have seen me display my best, what unique value did I create?

The results inspire a sense of pride, joy, and appreciation from the person being evaluated. Emerging themes encourage them to see what strengths others see in them, what people value, and their unique contributions. This helps them to create a "best-self portrait." A similar value-added feedback exercise is when colleagues are asked to intentionally give unique and positive feedback to one another. As a result, this creates a spiral of positivity, where people spend more time focusing on their strengths than their weaknesses, and colleagues feel more positive about each other and thus work better.

Positive relationships at work: Good-quality, positive working relationships add tremendous value to the organization, as they increase team bonding, connectivity, trust, wellbeing, and our ways of working with colleagues. According to Cameron (2008), they are also associated with less stress, higher levels of energy and productivity, more team and individual engagement, and more learning and promotional opportunities. Positive emotions and acts of kindness that stem from good relationships at work are paramount to feeling a sense of belonging. Research shows that positive relationships and good quality connections at work also affect our health in terms of reducing stress, improving our immune system, and even lowering blood pressure. These advantages have ripple effects from a business perspective on the individuals that work there, but also in the community and society. Implementing strategically planned and measurable activities that promote connectivity is another way of using positive psychology to build a successful business. This results in thriving communities.

Positive psychology workplace interventions: One way to encourage employee engagement is through applying positive psychology interventions (PPIs) to the workplace. According to authors and scientists in positive psychology, Parks and Biswas-Diener, a PPI addresses a positive psychology construct and has a body of research supporting its effectiveness. An intervention can be considered positive if the goal of the intervention is to improve rather than to remediate. PPIs are designed to promote positivity in people's everyday life, and by doing so, they help them cope with the adverse events and moods they might experience. For example, projects that promote kindness and mindfulness are considered PPIs.

Employees experiencing positive emotions through applying PPIs at work may become more emotionally engaged. This affects individual employees as well as other employees' motivation and emotions. This has a positive influence on organizations, both on the human as well as on the business side. However, before we as leaders facilitate interventions with our teams, we must acknowledge that the first intervention is with ourselves. As Piers Worth, a respected member of the Faculty of Society and Health at Buckinghamshire New University, proposes in the opening chapter of Proctor's *Positive Psychology Interventions in Practice*, we must bring qualities of attention, openness, and a willingness to suspend personal prior experiences. He continues to say that it is in finding and understanding oneself, through practicing interpersonal awareness, that we become prepared to 'intervene' with others.

SOME PRACTICAL EXAMPLES OF PPIS

There are several PPIs that you can implement at work. One PPI is setting an organizational strategy to support and cultivate wellbeing. This includes ensuring policies are aligned with wellbeing principles: enabling employees to utilize their strengths, setting SMART goals, creating opportunities for flow, and fostering meaningful social relationships. It also includes being mindful of people's values and beliefs when creating employee engagement programs and cultivating positive emotions through activities. Chapter 11 looks at wellbeing in detail.

GRATITUDE

Another PPI is a gratitude intervention, where colleagues are encouraged to be mindful, to feel and express gratitude through techniques such as journaling and feedback sessions to people they are grateful to. One highly successful gratitude intervention that I helped lead was a two-month holistic campaign that included:

- senior leaders creating a beautiful video to thank all colleagues for sticking by them and for their trust, loyalty, and commitment (during the month-long COVID-19 lockdown in the UAE)
- all employees being encouraged to submit up to three homemade creative gratitude cards to an individual or a team, thanking them for something specific they had done
- all internal communication platforms educating employees about the importance of gratitude and encouraging them to show appreciation daily.

HUMOR AND RESILIENCE

To increase wellbeing and create greater social and psychological capital, there are also some exciting studies that talk about humor PPIs, where humor training and intervention programs are introduced to the team to help generate laughter; increase positive affect, life satisfaction, and happy thoughts; and decrease negative affect and depression. Other PPIs could be used to build resilience, mental toughness, mindfulness, kindness, compassion, and connection. Resilient organizations, for instance, are seen to maintain a high level of performance during times of uncertainty, extreme pressures (such as those brought about during the COVID-19 pandemic), and threats. Prioritizing these PPIs will depend on the organizational culture, the industry, employees' personalities, and the country's culture.

CHARACTER STRENGTHS SPOTTING

Organizations can also introduce strengths spotting and nurture character strengths. Identifying and developing individuals' strengths is a compelling approach to promoting positivity at work. A person's strength is what they are naturally good at and enjoy doing. As McQuaid and Lawn (2015) describe it, utilizing our strengths enables performance at an optimal level. Research shows that when we work from our strengths, we are much less stressed, experience fewer negative emotions, and are more productive.

Peterson and his colleagues (2010) found that individuals whose strengths include spirituality, zest, gratitude, and hope are most often associated with greater job satisfaction across various industries. Thus, one may wonder to what extent your personality type or strengths affect your engagement levels at work. To learn more about your strengths, refer to tools such as the VIA Survey, CliftonStrengths (previously Gallup StrengthsFinder), or Realise2. These tools help individuals assess their strengths and put them into perspective. It is also worth noting that Biswas-Diener and colleagues (2011) encourage people to find their 'golden mean,' which helps individuals develop the right strengths in the right amounts and situations. Through research, McQuaid (2015) found that managers who focus on their employees' strengths considerably decrease active disengagement; similarly, those leaders who focus on their employees' weaknesses have witnessed significant decreases in their performance.

POSITIVE ENERGY NETWORKS

Research by Owen and colleagues (2016) proposes that people can be characterized as 'positive' or 'negative' energizers. Positive energizers help bring the organization to life. Negative energizers deplete feelings of enthusiasm and happiness in the organization. The good news is that 'positive energizing' is actually a learned behavior! Businesses can therefore create PPIs that foster and encourage people with positive energy to help boost their personal and organizational productivity and accelerate the contributions of their teammates. Identifying and empowering positive energizers is vital for POS, cultural change, positive energy, and employee engagement.

IMPLICATIONS FOR POSITIVE PSYCHOLOGY AT WORK

Emphasizing positively deviant workplaces is not something new. For more than thirty years, organizations have been using positive psychology practices, and what is important to remember is that change strategies must align with organizational values. According to Froman (2010) and Mills and colleagues (2013), critical factors for a successful organizational change strategy include an excellent company structure; supportive and empowering leadership;

and defined behaviors, capabilities, policies, systems, processes, and social support. For positive organizational change to occur, individuals must be united in understanding the direction the organization needs to take. They must also work together to establish the necessary environment for this change to take place. Their resilience, perseverance, and ability to authentically connect with members of the workforce will determine the extent of their success. In addition, change takes time and must be a collaborative movement with various organizational stakeholders.

This chapter provided a good understanding of the concept of positive psychology and, more specifically, positive workplaces and how to create them. We plunged into several practical applications influenced by positive organizational scholarship with the intention of building positive organizational behavior. We reviewed the evolution of economic to human to social capital and discussed how to create positive psychological capital amongst colleagues by building hope, optimism, self-efficacy, and resilience. Essential concepts such as positive emotions, best-self feedback, appreciative inquiry, and positive leadership were discussed, and we also explored the power of PPIs at work.

I sincerely hope that this introduction to positive psychology and how it can be used to build a thriving and flourishing organization has inspired you to look at your workplace through a different set of eyes and has sparked excitement about this field of psychology. I hope you will be encouraged to adapt or implement some of the discussed interventions. To guide you further on this, the next chapter will focus on positive communication, providing you with a methodology to improve internal communication in the workplace.

CHALLENGE ACCEPTED: PUTTING *POSITIVE WORKPLACES* INTO ACTION

Try these suggested activities, experiment, have fun, and explore the endless possibilities of applying PPIs to create a more fulfilling work experience for your organization.

1. Strengths Synergy Challenge

Task: Each team member takes a personal strengths assessment and shares their top three strengths with their department.

Challenge: Brainstorm ways to combine individual strengths into powerful team synergies. Identify projects, tasks, or challenges where employees can leverage their strengths collaboratively.

Activity: Assign roles within the team based on identified strengths and synergies. Monitor progress and celebrate successes that showcase teamwork.

2. Positive Psychology Intervention Design Lab

Task: Assign each department a specific PPI, such as gratitude exercises or strengths-focused activities.

Challenge: Design an engaging way to implement the PPI within the work environment. Think beyond traditional methods and consider fun and interactive approaches.

Activity: Have each group present their designed PPI intervention. Celebrate creativity and share ideas for implementing and adapting these interventions within the company.

3. Engaging Leadership Bingo

Task: Create a bingo card with squares representing positive leadership behaviors (e.g., providing feedback, showing appreciation, recognizing achievements). Employees observe leaders and mark squares when they witness these behaviors.

Challenge: Encourage active observation and appreciation for positive leadership actions. This shifts the focus from expecting to actively seeking and acknowledging effective leadership practices.

Activity: Once a bingo is achieved, encourage group discussions about the observed behaviors and their impact on teamwork, motivation, and overall engagement. This promotes awareness of positive leadership and inspires others to emulate effective practices. You can also reward the leaders who display the most positive leadership attributes in one month.

CHAPTER 9

INTERNAL COMMUNICATION

"Like a human being, a company has to have an internal communication mechanism, a 'nervous system,' to coordinate its actions."

—BILL GATES

Effective communication is fundamental to the continuous success of organizations, and fostering a culture inspired by excellent internal communication (IC) will undoubtedly contribute toward a thriving and engaged work environment.

This chapter will give an overview of IC and everything you need to know about it. It includes a complete framework and strategy to help you connect with, engage, and influence your team's knowledge, attitudes, and behaviors for maximum benefit. You will learn about the role and purpose of IC, its benefits to the organization, and how this relates to the overall employee experience. By the end of this chapter, you will have a deeper understanding of workplace IC and how you can organize and utilize your resources to improve the quality of communications. Additionally, you will be equipped with the knowledge of how to shape engaging communications channels within your organization so that you can positively influence the employee experience and drive financial results. Engaged and informed colleagues are a company's best asset, and IC is the structure that holds the company together.

According to research conducted in 2017 by the Chartered Institute of Public Relations in conjunction with the Institute of Internal Communication, there is a clear link between good IC and an organization's financial success. One reason for this is that superb IC is one of the strongest drivers of employee engagement and employee experience. The role of IC is to ensure a high level of alignment and understanding throughout the organization, which in turn enables meaningful connections at work. Meaningful connections are part of the makeup of social wellbeing, and as you may know, employee wellbeing strongly influences the health of an organization. So, to have a healthy, thriving, and profitable workplace, organizations must ensure that their internal and external communication is outstanding. Both are essential elements and critical aspects of daily operations and should be key focus areas of any business or industry. Let's begin this section by looking at what internal communication is.

WHAT IS INTERNAL COMMUNICATION?

Let's look at how some academics and prominent practitioners define it. For starters, make a mental note of the difference between *internal communication* (the way a company communicates) and *internal communications* (the tools, tactics, and channels used to communicate).

It is also crucial to understand the difference between internal and external communication.

Internal communication serves to guide and unite colleagues at all levels through communication across various corporate channels on a regular basis.

External communication aims to shape society's viewpoint about the company through social media, press releases, conferences, etc. on a regular basis.

Just as external communication must be flawless, well-planned, and engaging, so should internal communication. Remember, when something is communicated internally, it becomes subject to potential external communication. The two areas of communication should be aligned and work in harmony to promote a consistent brand and employer-brand message.

Rachel Miller, a renowned figure in the field of internal communication, defines IC as "the way a company interacts with its people and [the way] they interact with it." This is a very simple definition, but it encompasses the entirety of the term. I am heavily influenced and inspired by Rachel Miller, and I am glad to be able to include some of her insights here.

Two other authorities on the subject, Tench and Yeomans (2006), say that IC is "the planned use of communication actions to systematically influence the knowledge, attitudes, and behaviors of current employees."

Elsewhere, the Institute of Internal Communication proposes that:

"Organizations need to communicate effectively with their employees. It sounds simple, but the reality is less so. And as organizations get bigger, this becomes a more complex challenge. At the most basic level, you have to communicate well at the right time so employees know what is expected of them and what is happening in the organization. At a deeper level, for employees to feel engaged with their workplace and give their best, they have to believe their organization cares about their views and understand how their role contributes towards overall business objectives."

I look at IC as the Fourth Estate of the corporate world. Now, I know that *the Fourth Estate*, a term coined by British historian Thomas

Carlyle, symbolizes the media or the press, an institution and segment of society that directly influences the masses. It partners with three other branches of government: the legislative, executive, and judicial branches. In some countries, the other three estates are considered the nobility, the Church, and the common people. The media is often referred to as one of the pillars of democracy because it disseminates information to people and is associated with freedom of expression. This pillar, or estate, is essential to a country's political, economic, and international affairs.

How IC can influence an organization is similar (although on a smaller scale) to the way media can influence the public. Therefore, the role of someone who oversees IC is extremely crucial. It holds a high degree of responsibility.

Although there may be a designation within the business for an IC practitioner or an IC department, everybody participates in the act of IC and creates a three-way communication flow—but why three-way?

The downward or top-down approach: senior leadership shares information with colleagues. This can be done through a post on the company intranet, a town-hall meeting, or a video from the CEO. This approach is generally one-directional. To foster trust, leaders must ensure that their communication is factual, detailed, readily available, timely, honest, and empathetic.

The upward or bottom-up approach: the flow of information from colleagues to management. This channel must always be kept open, and stakeholders' opinions from various demographics must be engaged through methods such as design thinking to ensure a good flow. Examples include surveys, direct comments during casual conversations, suggestion boxes, focus groups, and one-on-one interviews.

And **the horizontal or sideways approach**: the flow of messages between employees and departments to each other. Good horizontal communication is created through networking, teamwork, trust, cooperation, and understanding. Companies must provide digital platforms and organize social events, team building, and celebrations to foster this. Additionally, creating the right office environment and physical space also matters immensely.

Internal communication is not merely about sending information out by email and communicating 'to' colleagues, 'at' colleagues, and talking down to them. It is instead about communicating *with* people and ensuring the entire process is smooth, ethical, and conducive to honesty without negative repercussions.

WHAT IS INTERNAL COMMUNICATION FOR?

As Miller defines it, the purpose of IC is:

"Not telling people what to do.
It is to create a shared understanding and
meaning. Only when this happens can employees
work together towards a company's goals."

The core purpose is to set a clear vision and an unobstructed path to reach that vision so that employees know what they are working towards and are empowered to get there. It serves to engage people, unite them, help create a sense of meaning and purpose for what they do, lead, grow, and develop. It serves to deliver change.

As Grossman says:

"Internal communications' function is to help leaders in your department or agency inform and engage employees, in a way which motivates staff to maximize their performance and deliver the business strategy most effectively. It is not about 'sending out stuff'."

From my experience, IC's purpose is to give a voice to every employee. It should aim to facilitate a relationship between all stakeholders in a company. Good IC means that 'the message' has touched people and has promoted dialogue. Good IC also helps employees see the big picture; it empowers and motivates them. It provides a roadmap to the mission and the company's vision and shows people how they all fit in. But it doesn't need to be as deep as this; on a basic level, good IC provides information and sets the standards. It fosters a culture of honesty, integrity, and trust, all of which are vital to business continuity and community success.

This drives business success through high employee engagement and a strong sense of loyalty. It creates powerful and continuous employee advocacy where the employees, also considered potentially the most credible brand ambassadors, say amazing things about their employers. Effective communication helps to drive productivity and innovation. It creates memorable and transformational customer experiences. Ultimately, great IC is responsible for a great employee experience. So, how do you do great internal communication?

THE ROAD TO A GREAT INTERNAL COMMUNICATION STRATEGY

Earlier in this chapter, I mentioned that all the employees of a company are responsible for IC because they all partake in it. Some of the key stakeholders that drive IC are the CEO and the senior leadership team, the HR leaders, and other business unit managers. The higher up you are in the organization, the more influence you have over the tone and style of the communication culture.

There should be a caretaker of the strategy: a choir conductor who sets the tone for the intended tune. I love how one guest explains the role of an IC practitioner in Rachel Miller's Podcast, *Candid Comms*: he talks about the conductor (the internal comms professional) in an orchestra directing everyone through music and notes. This person typically sits within the HR department, but sometimes they may also be part of the marketing or PR team, the corporate team, or even a team on their own directly reporting to the CEO. This is someone who absolutely must have a great relationship with the senior leadership team. Regardless of where the IC function sits, it's essential to have a great strategy that is derived from company values and goals and that has the buy-in of the senior leadership team.

A well-formed strategy clearly defines your goals: what, why, and how you communicate with colleagues. A strategy helps you see the big picture when planning the activities required to achieve these goals. This roadmap takes you on a successful IC journey. A successful IC journey ultimately leads to informed, motivated, productive, and loyal employees who will say good things about your company and go above and beyond to help achieve collective success.

It is essential to consider the opposite of a good IC strategy, which is a bad one (or none)! Lack of IC—or a poorly structured, planned, and directed strategy—has negative repercussions. Communication helps to unite people toward a common purpose. A poorly executed IC strategy may lead to disgruntlement, cultural entropy, mistrust, team conflict, and low morale. This harms the employee experience, the guest experience, and company productivity and profits in the long run. Poor IC creates a bad company culture.

The foundation of every great strategy, communication calendar, campaign, and message must address fundamental questions. My journalism degree from the University of Malta crucially taught us to consider the following essentials when planning communication. In journalism, these are called the 5Ws and the 1H. These can be used to create a matrix for the overall plan, but they may also be used if you launch a campaign or ask for feedback. Great messages usually satisfy the audience by answering all these questions. The quality of your life depends on the quality of your questions. And so, let's begin to break this down. Remember, we aim to foster three-way communication, so you should always make room for dialogue.

#1 Why are you doing what you are doing? What is your objective? What is your end goal? Is it done with the purpose of employee engagement, retention, change management, and awesome customer experiences? What about your company's bottom-line performance, profitability, and productivity? What about not-for-profit companies?

The rest will easily follow once you define your objectives and purpose!

BEYOND EMPLOYEE ENGAGEMENT

#2 Who is your audience, and is your message relevant to them? How do you get them to hear it amid hundreds and thousands of other 'messages' competing for their attention every day? The audience should be segmented by demographics.

#3 What do you want your audience to *know, think, feel, say,* and *do* because of your message? What should they do about your message? Look at it from their perspective. What type of feedback are you looking to receive: qualitative or quantitative?

#4 When do you intend to deliver the message? Timing your messages is crucial. I'm not just talking about the time of the day when most people access social media, such as when they go for lunch and have time to browse the company intranet or look at noticeboards. I'm also talking about aligning your message with everything else that is going on in the organization and competing against you. What is the 'temperature' like in the company at the time when you are announcing happy news and promotions? Are you sensitive to the company's energy and how employees may feel two weeks after a big round of redundancies? Is it really the right time to launch a sports festival? What is the frequency: is it hourly, daily, bi-weekly, weekly, monthly? What time of the day, or which day of the week? Information sending and information gathering must be timely. There is no point in asking for feedback on an event a month after it has finished.

Communication must not appear sporadic and unplanned. Some messages will need to be more frequent, whilst others can be gathered over the course of a month or a quarter.

#5 Where is your audience? Are they working onsite, remotely, or is there a hybrid working arrangement?

#6 How many people would you like to reach? Where would you like to communicate, and on which channels? This depends on the message and on the audience. How would you like to receive feedback? Verbal, written, instantaneous? That's when social media, an intranet, and company apps are beneficial. When communicating company-side messages, it is best to use all the media channels you've got: town-hall meetings, daily briefings, company newsletters, emails, instant messages, the intranet, noticeboards, videos, podcasts, etc. Something else I love is repurposing messages. For instance, when doing a live in-person town-hall meeting, it's always best to record (audio and video), and from there, you can do many things, like:

- turn parts of it into a podcast
- resend the live recording to those who couldn't attend
- generate the minutes of the meeting and send them out together with the presentation that was used during the meeting
- create posters of the most essential discussion points
- save the videos and do a year-end compilation of all the best bits as a reminder of how the year went.

Did it work? This is something we often forget to evaluate. Always consider a mixed approach, including both qualitative and quantitative measurements. Are people opening and reading your weekly email newsletters? Is there participation in your Q&A session during the town-hall meeting? Are colleagues answering a survey truthfully? What are they doing because of your newest wellbeing campaign? What do they say to each other over lunch?

ORGANIZATIONAL VALUES AND THE INTERNAL COMMUNICATION STRATEGY

Other essential elements that should be considered when laying the groundwork for an IC strategy are the company values, mission, vision, purpose, employee value proposition, and annual goals. The values must be at the heart of the IC strategy, and they should continuously guide and inspire messages, campaigns, competitions, activations, and events. Company vision, mission, and purpose will ideally be used throughout all company communication because this demonstrates that the company authentically lives its values and mission and encourages employees to do the same. Understanding how internal messages fit as part of the overall purpose helps to create a more meaningful and authentic work environment. This drives commitment and engagement and shapes the employee experience.

It is paramount for colleagues to be inspired by and to behave according to an organization's values. This helps to shape the company culture and bring it to life. Thus, basing your IC strategy on values is a principal first step. An IC plan must also be aligned with the overall business strategy and objectives. In doing so, a good IC strategy builds trust and understanding and helps connect colleagues to a common vision and purpose.

BENEFITS OF INTERNAL COMMUNICATION

Here is an excellent diagram borrowed from TalkFreely's article, "Internal Communication ... Everything you need to know."

IT'S THE LAW!

So, you don't have a choice. There will be times when you have to communicate to comply with legislation, such as around health & safety, pensions or paternity rights.

ADVOCACY

Helping people say the right things about the organisation to family and friends. Keeping the Brand Promise and satisfying customers.

CHANGE

Communication provides the glue for Senior Management's change, engagement and transformation programes. It is essential for cultural evolution and the delivery of organisational results.

EFFECTIVENESS

Improving organisational effectiveness through collaboration, creating a better work environment and empowering middle management. Providing communication training, and developing new communication technologies.

RETENTION

Keeping good staff by giving them positive motivators to stay and enjoy their work. Showing them how they personally, and the business more widely, are making a difference.

UNDERSTANDING

Helping everyone understand and share in the strategy, vision and values of the organisation. Being transparent about challenges and limiting rumours during times of crisis.

ENGAGEMENT

It helps organisations engage employees by encouraging two-way dialogue so that staff feel their views count. Making leaders more visible and accessible to employees to show they are listening.

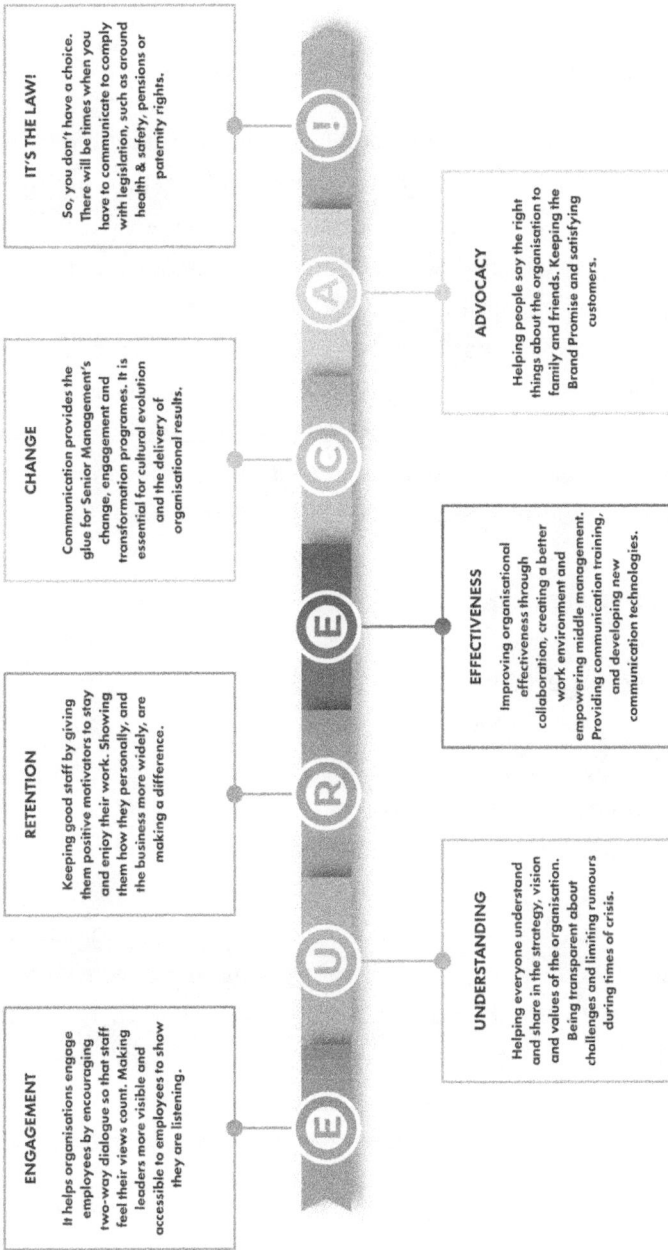

FIGURE 8. THE BENEFITS OF INTERNAL COMMUNICATION

HOW TO CREATE AN INTERNAL COMMUNICATION STRATEGY

Now that we have discussed what IC is, who is responsible for it, and what its purpose is, we will review the key objectives of an IC strategy and the various channels and activities one may use, as well as the communication and engagement metrics that will help guide you in implementing it.

An IC strategy is like a roadmap for your organization's journey. Ideally, it should involve all key stakeholders' opinions and guidance and be employee-centric. Miller addresses this very succinctly through her award-winning *All Things IC* blog. Before beginning to plan that journey, you must assess:

- where you are now
- where you're heading (objectives)
- how you'll get there
- how long will it take
- what's involved to get there
- why this approach is suitable
- how you'll know when you've reached the goal (measurement).

Miller proposes that the *what* and the *why* are the strategic questions, whilst the *how*, *where*, and *when* are more practical. These seven questions will give you clarity and purpose.

Earlier, I discussed some of the objectives of IC, which were to inform, educate, unite, give meaning and purpose, engage, understand, and be understood. Another key objective is to make positive change.

Here are some great infographics that summarize some of what I just discussed. I have personally used them for strategy creation, and they are fabulous! All credit goes to Rachel Miller and *Alive with Ideas,* who created these wonderful infographics.

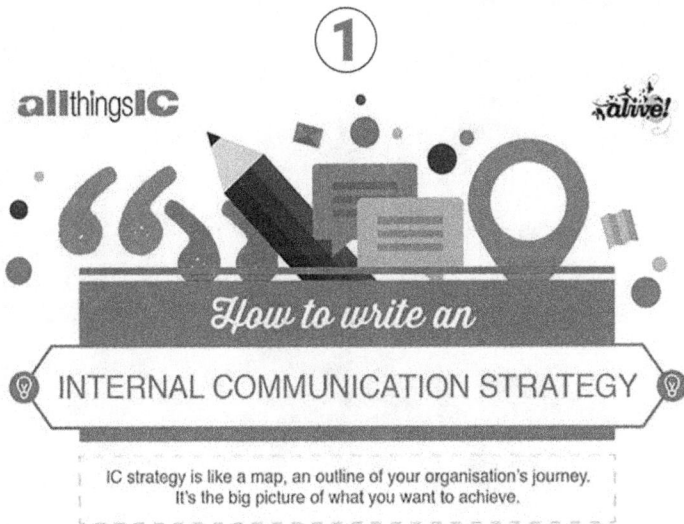

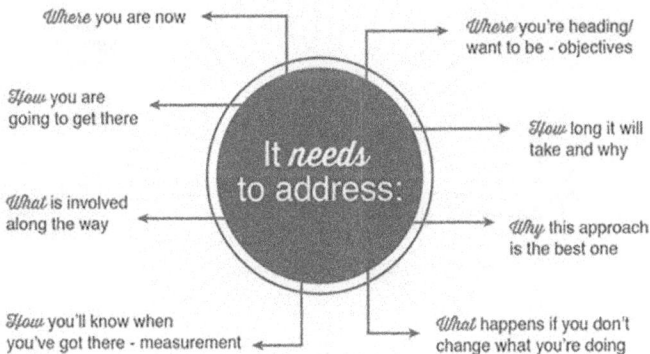

(1)

allthings**IC**

alive!

How to write an
INTERNAL COMMUNICATION STRATEGY

IC strategy is like a map, an outline of your organisation's journey. It's the big picture of what you want to achieve.

Where you are now

Where you're heading/ want to be - objectives

How you are going to get there

It *needs* to address:

How long it will take and why

What is involved along the way

Why this approach is the best one

How you'll know when you've got there - measurement

What happens if you don't change what you're doing

Your strategy is how you capture all this information so everyone knows what route the company is taking, how they fit in, why this approach is best and how you're going to get to your destination.

②

What *should* be included?

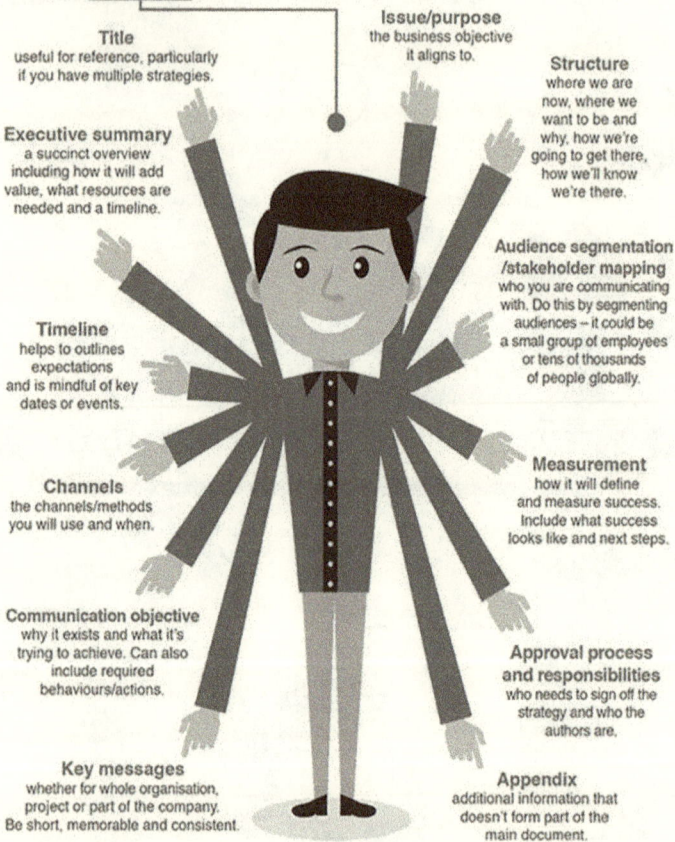

Issue/purpose
the business objective
it aligns to.

Title
useful for reference, particularly
if you have multiple strategies.

Structure
where we are
now, where we
want to be and
why, how we're
going to get there,
how we'll know
we're there.

Executive summary
a succinct overview
including how it will add
value, what resources are
needed and a timeline.

**Audience segmentation
/stakeholder mapping**
who you are communicating
with. Do this by segmenting
audiences – it could be
a small group of employees
or tens of thousands
of people globally.

Timeline
helps to outlines
expectations
and is mindful of key
dates or events.

Measurement
how it will define
and measure success.
Include what success
looks like and next steps.

Channels
the channels/methods
you will use and when.

Communication objective
why it exists and what it's
trying to achieve. Can also
include required
behaviours/actions.

**Approval process
and responsibilities**
who needs to sign off the
strategy and who the
authors are.

Key messages
whether for whole organisation,
project or part of the company.
Be short, memorable and consistent.

Appendix
additional information that
doesn't form part of the
main document.

(3)

What format should it be in?

Some companies use written docs like Word, some presentations, while others use spreadsheets.

Tip
It should be a living document, accessible by others. If using Word/PDF, consider including bookmarks to help readers navigate through the content.

How long should it be?

Strategies vary from 2-4 sides of A4 to 10-15 pages or more.

Some longer strategies include elements like a channels matrix, stakeholder mapping and feedback from relevant sources like employee surveys or audits.

Tip
Shorter is better if you want it to be read and actioned.

Who should write it?

IC strategies are often written by an IC pro as they're closest to understanding the priorities.

This can be someone internally or an expert who is called in to offer advice and guidance.

Tip
Involve others when appropriate to help get buy-in, e.g. external comms colleagues and business partners such as HR, Legal, IT.

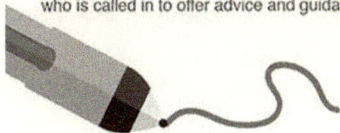

④

What should *you consider?* ←

At the heart of your strategy should be what you want employees to do/say/think/feel differently

The key word is clarity: about the particular project it relates to, area of the business or company as a whole, and how it aligns to your organisation's overall objectives.

Ensure you have qualitative and quantitative information - understand the reality of communication in your company through audit results, anecdotal feedback, employee surveys/ focus group feedback.

The more directly you can tailor the content and appeal to each group, the better chance of success you have in achieving what you're setting out to do.

Keep language simple and easy to understand. Packing it full of jargon does no one any favours!

Measurement is key to understanding what good looks like, how to know what's working and when you've achieved your objectives.

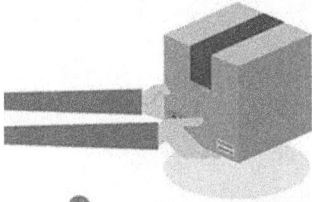

FIGURE 9. HOW TO WRITE AN INTERNAL COMMUNICATION STRATEGY

A FOUR-WAY COMMUNICATION METHODOLOGY: CHANNELS AND ACTIVITIES

Choosing the right channels for personalized communication distribution and gathering feedback is essential to ensuring a successful IC culture. It's imperative to understand how to reach employees according to their preferences. You may wish to communicate by email with office staff, but you might want to adopt a digital platform if you are looking at an audience who does not use a computer regularly, does not have a company email address, or is geographically spread out. With so many ways of communicating, it is crucial for IC practitioners to select the appropriate combination of methods that foster four-way communication. This is called 'omnichannel communication.'

Until now, I have been talking about three-way communication (downward, upward, horizontal), but it's time to add another layer and emphasize four-way communication. This is, namely, the informal way. Informal communication occurs outside of the pre-established channels of transmitting information. Shoobridge, a scholar and known figure in the field of IC, talks about this mode being somewhat dangerous, as it's often based on gossip and rumors and may not necessarily be true. But, if managed well, Shoobridge notes that "it can help establish better human relations among employees within the organization and can also positively supplement formal corporate communications."

Innovisor, a company that helps leaders prioritize and accelerate commitment to their communication strategies, coined the "Three Percent Rule." It identifies the informal influencers inside organizations. Their research and business suggest that 3% of people shape the perceptions of up to 90%!

In my fascinating interview with Richard Lalleman, Head of Learning, Innovation, and Quality at Innovisor, he affirmed that the #ThreePercentRule is a small group of individuals within the organization that shape the emotions of the larger mass, and this critical stakeholder group accelerates mindset change. Through their innovative research methodology, Lalleman empowers businesses to succeed by hacking the world of informal communication, informal organizational dynamics, and hidden networks. He is part of a team that advises clients on who the people with the informal influence are, how to partner with them, and how the influence flows throughout the organization via informal influence networks.

This knowledge enables IC professionals and senior leaders to engage the right people in the right tasks to achieve their IC objectives and business goals. These individuals could also be the informal cheerleaders discussed in the chapter on culture.

Let's look at some recommended methods you can use to foster a four-way communication strategy.

Table 2. Fostering Four-Way Communication

Traditional Communication	Digital Communication	Personable Communication	Information-Gathering Tools	Informal Tools for Communication
Print news-letters/ magazines/ leaflets/ letters/ noticeboards	Video messages and video magazines	Face-to-face live town-hall meetings	Surveys assessing employee experience	Informal influencers
Company radio	Employee apps, platforms, intranet	Leadership meetings	Pulse questions and polls	Through the grapevine: gossip and rumors
Posters and billboards	Live-streamed virtual and hybrid town-hall meetings	One-on-one discussions	Focus groups	Back channels
Reward & recognition ceremonies/ through a speech at such an event	Email	Daily team briefings/ communication champions	Entry/stay/ exit interviews	Through external sources not working in the company

Traditional Communi-cation	Digital Communi-cation	Personable Communi-cation	Information-Gathering Tools	Informal Tools for Communi-cation
Customer feedback about the service provided, the level of exper-tise and engagement	Social media/ Zoom/ Teams/ teleconfer-encing tools	Word of mouth/ anecdotal feedback	eNPS (employee net pro-moter score)	
Thank-you cards	Blogs	Annual goals, per-formance appraisals, personal develop-ment plans	Physical or digital suggestion boxes	
Company-wide campaigns	Podcasts/ audio messages/ webinars/ company radio	Team building/ social events	Competi-tions where employees can submit ideas and win prizes	

LISTENING TO YOUR EMPLOYEES IS NOT AN ANNUAL AFFAIR

Now that you know what *good* IC is about, let's take it a level higher. What makes IC *great* is effective listening. I wonder how often your organization listens to its employees—yearly, bi-yearly, quarterly? How many can answer 'daily' to this question? How often do you take the time to actively listen to the voice of employees, and how often do you respond to that voice with desirable actions?

COMMUNICATION METRICS

It's imperative to assess the effectiveness of your communication, and you must keep in mind the downward, upward, horizontal, and informal communication flows when assessing it. These four interactions provide a holistic picture of how well the company keeps its people informed, engaged, aligned, and empowered to give feedback across all levels. It also tells you what you must continue doing, stop doing, or change. Good measurement provides evidence for return on investment. To monitor the effectiveness of IC, I propose using a variety of methods, such as:

- monitoring participation/usage
- checking click-through and read rates
- survey response rates
- monitoring attendance at an event
- total reach and employee participation
- employee engagement scores.

However, the effectiveness of your communication as measured through click-through rates, attendance, usage, and surveys is somewhat irrelevant if it does not drive behavior. For that, you would need to analyze:

- performance rates
- employee loyalty

- employee retention percentages
- customer comments and experiences.

Remember, what do you want people to think, know, feel, say, and do because of your messages? Most metrics validate what people think, know, and feel (if they are being truthful). Is your workforce actually doing it, or is it just saying it?

The chapter on metrics includes more information on measuring the efficacy of IC and how it affects the overall employee experience.

A FEW TIPS TO SET YOURSELF UP FOR SUCCESS

1. Monitor the effectiveness and engagement of your communication (through desired behaviors and software).
2. Ensure you have created avenues for feedback, allowing colleagues to respond or discuss.
3. Remember the length, complexity, and language used; keep everything simple and avoid acronyms, technical language, and jargon.
4. Make communication regular and timely; if the town hall is set to begin at 2.00 pm, don't begin at 2.45 pm.
5. Connect personally and authentically with your teams daily and weekly. Technology isn't enough to assess your employees' sentiment and energy. Remember, communication isn't about 'sending stuff out'. As leaders, we are accountable for regularly checking the pulse of the organization.

6. How does our strategy change if there is a more diverse and disparate workforce, working from multiple locations?
7. From a neurodiversity perspective, consider how each recipient will interpret your message. Adapt your communication tone and style to cater to the majority, not the minority.
8. Engage communication champions, informal influencers, and departmental managers to ensure your messages are communicated effectively.

AND FINALLY ...

Done well, internal communication gives employees a voice. It drives change. It also creates alignment between colleagues' work-life, purpose, and meaning. When the *why* is clear, the *how* is easy. I hope this chapter gave you a rich understanding of the crucial role and purpose of IC in terms of employee engagement and the employee experience. Companies that invest time, energy, and resources into fostering meaningful four-way communication and connections build positive interpersonal relationships, trust, and authentic employee engagement. By understanding what makes a great IC strategy and genuinely following the guidance in this chapter, you will reap tremendous rewards that result in organizational productivity, profitability, and greater workplace efficiencies. You will create an inspirational organization that offers an unforgettable customer experience.

And now, let's set off to the next chapter, where you will learn about the magical power of meaningful rewards and recognition.

CHALLENGE ACCEPTED: PUTTING *INTERNAL COMMS* INTO ACTION

Here are some suggested activities that will help improve internal communication in your organization. Enjoy!

1. Internal Communication Audit Challenge

Task: Divide employees into teams and assign each team a specific IC channel (e.g., email, intranet, team meetings, social platforms).

Challenge: Analyze the effectiveness of the assigned channel, and ask the employees to identify strengths, weaknesses, and areas for improvement.

Activity: Have each team present their findings and recommendations for enhancing the channel's effectiveness. Implement the best ideas to improve overall IC.

2. Feedback Flip Day

Task: Dedicate a day where employees actively seek and give constructive feedback to colleagues, both upwards and downwards. Encourage using a specific framework for providing feedback like the *Start, Stop, Continue* method.

Challenge: Focus on actionable and specific feedback that helps individuals and teams improve. Create a safe space for open dialogue and ensure everyone feels comfortable giving and receiving feedback.

Activity: Share key learnings and suggestions for improvement gathered during the day. Implement action plans based on the collected feedback.

3. Communication Champion Challenge

Task: Select Communication Champions from different departments to champion effective IC practices.

Challenge: Empower champions to organize communication-focused activities, provide feedback on internal channels, and act as peer-to-peer communication coaches.

Activity: Provide champions with training and resources to excel in their role. Reward and recognize their contributions and showcase their successes to encourage wider participation.

CHAPTER 10

MOTIVATION, PRIDE, AND REWARDS AND RECOGNITION

*"The reason that leaders are interested in what moti-
vates employees is that motivation leads to commitment,
commitment leads to engagement and engagement
leads to high performance."*

— THE BARRETT VALUES CENTRE

A few years ago, I was in a position where I could afford the down payment for a beautiful three-bedroom townhouse in a gated community that was under construction in Dubai. I was offered an attractive payment plan directly from the developer, meaning I didn't need to take out a home loan and pay interest rates. So, I took the opportunity and purchased the property while it was still being constructed.

My circumstances at the time of purchase quickly changed with the onset of COVID-19, and I found myself in a precarious position where maintaining the ambitious payment plan had become a challenge. With a 20% reduction in salary plus the looming danger of losing my job any minute, I began to feel the stress and panic of having to pay for a villa I was not even living in! Looking for a higher-paying job was futile because most industries were at a standstill or downsizing. Until then, I had never been motivated by a high salary (although I was in a director position). I am proud of the extra time and effort I devote to my career. My unwavering commitment and genuine care have allowed me to bring positive change to the lives of those I work with. Unfortunately, my new predicament and tight financial situation could not be ignored. Motivated purely by the possibility of a higher salary, better benefits, and stock options, I sought higher-paid opportunities.

Understanding this chapter is imperative to building a strong foundation for the employee experience. It is the secret ingredient needed to build a high-performing organization. Here, we focus on comprehending what motivates individuals to perform at their best, what encourages them to feel a sense of pride in their work and their organization, and what leaders can do to facilitate appropriate appreciation, rewards, and recognition for employees' invaluable input.

Throughout this chapter, we will look at several psychological theories regarding motivation and pride. In a positive and thriving work environment, the factors that inspire and drive employees exceed those that discourage or demotivate them. There are multiple factors behind what motivates people. They can be as varied as having fun at work, having variety in projects, being empowered to make decisions, teamwork, having clear goals, and the ability to use your strengths and grow. On the other hand, there are many reasons someone can become demotivated at work. These include organizational politics, dishonesty and lack of accountability, constant change, a culture of blame, poor and invisible leadership, unfairness, and perceived inequality. Sometimes, a company can tick all the boxes in terms of its employee experience, but personal circumstances can take precedence, no matter how engaged an individual is.

Let's unpack some models for employee motivation and discuss why these psychological theories matter when creating a successful workplace. The first theory we're going to explore is the Motivation-Hygiene Theory.

Frederick Herzberg's **Motivation-Hygiene Theory** encourages people in supervisory, managerial, or leadership positions to engage in ongoing conversations with their employees to understand what they want from their work experience. According to him, two elements are involved in employee motivation and dissatisfaction, and both must be provided for in the workplace.

1. **Intrinsic motivation factors**, also called job satisfiers, are concepts such as enjoying the work, feeling a sense of growth, development, empowerment, responsibility, and ultimately feeling a sense of accomplishment. These factors motivate employees *intrinsically*, or from within.

2. **Hygiene factors** or extrinsic motivators include a well-designed physical work environment, a competitive salary and benefits, appropriate company policies, and meaningful relationships with others. If these needs are met and handled well, they do not necessarily *create* satisfaction or motivation, but they can *prevent* employee dissatisfaction. A well-designed physical environment may not necessarily motivate individuals to work harder, but terrible working conditions (dissatisfiers) may make people resign. Hygiene factors may cause dissatisfaction if they are missing from the workplace.

The **Job Characteristics Model** proposed by Oldham and Hackman states that work needs to be interesting for people to enjoy it and be motivated. According to this model, the ultimate sources of major demotivation can be monotonous work, tasks without meaning or purpose, lack of end goals, and work that is not challenging enough. Furthermore, employees who don't receive feedback on their work (either criticism or praise) quickly become demotivated.

Maslow's Hierarchy of Needs can also be applied in the workplace to help motivate employees. It presents a hierarchy of five levels:

1. The *physiological needs* of an individual must be met. These include safe working spaces, respect, equality, toilet facilities, drinking water, and a place to eat.
2. The second level highlights *emotional and psychological safety* and job security. Employees cannot feel motivated unless their most basic needs (level one and two) are fulfilled.
3. Once the basic needs are met, the third level for workplaces to 'get right' is the psychological need for belonging and love. These may be encouraged by creating opportunities for people to connect authentically and develop friendships.
4. *Esteem* is the fourth level. When applied to work, 'esteem' means that individuals must believe that they contribute to a higher goal and that their contributions are recognized. We will look at recognition and rewards extensively in the latter part of this chapter. Esteem is also built by growth and accomplishment. Motivation increases if this growth and accomplishment is encouraged and celebrated.
5. The final level is self-actualization or self-fulfillment. Once an individual has reached this stage, they have maximized their potential at work. Someone at this stage is generally sufficiently challenged, trusted, and empowered; this leads to growth and engagement.

This hierarchy model is my favorite because it factors in a multitude of levels of human complexity and reality.

Kegan's three types of mind suggest that people are motivated according to their current level of psychological development and their present life circumstances. The below image shows the seven stages of psychological development.

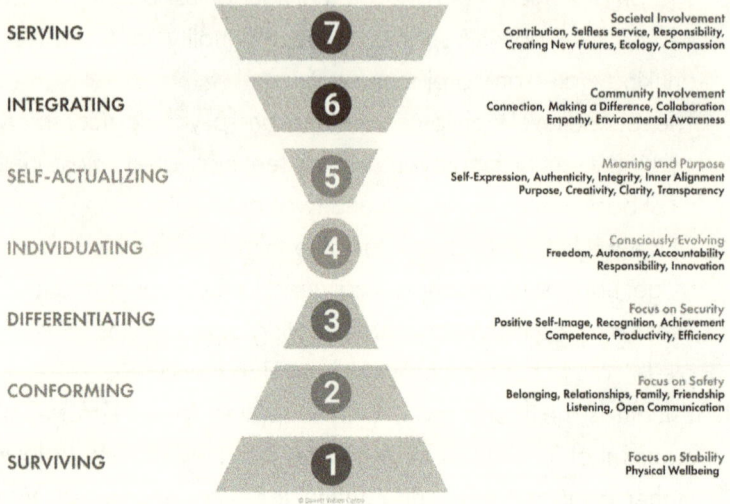

SERVING	7	Societal Involvement Contribution, Selfless Service, Responsibility, Creating New Futures, Ecology, Compassion
INTEGRATING	6	Community Involvement Connection, Making a Difference, Collaboration Empathy, Environmental Awareness
SELF-ACTUALIZING	5	Meaning and Purpose Self-Expression, Authenticity, Integrity, Inner Alignment Purpose, Creativity, Clarity, Transparency
INDIVIDUATING	4	Consciously Evolving Freedom, Autonomy, Accountability Responsibility, Innovation
DIFFERENTIATING	3	Focus on Security Positive Self-Image, Recognition, Achievement Competence, Productivity, Efficiency
CONFORMING	2	Focus on Safety Belonging, Relationships, Family, Friendship Listening, Open Communication
SURVIVING	1	Focus on Stability Physical Wellbeing

FIGURE 10. THE SEVEN STAGES OF PSYCHOLOGICAL DEVELOPMENT

Like Maslow's model, the first three stages focus on caring for our basic needs, belonging, and developing a sense of self-worth. The fourth and fifth stages center around satisfying our first-order growth needs: individuating and self-actualizing. The sixth and seventh stages focus on satisfying our second-order growth needs: integrating and serving.

Furthermore, according to Harvard scholars Kegan and Lahey, these seven stages can be divided into three plateaus of growth. Humans evolve from one level to another as our consciousness grows:

1. the socialized mind
2. the self-authoring mind
3. the self-transforming mind.

According to the Barrett Values Centre, the *socialized mind* is **dependent**. People of this mind want to fit in and say what they think people want to hear. They are unlikely to be motivated by the promise of a leadership role. They usually think of their work as a job and are highly engaged by their role. Their biggest motivators are incentives such as decent pay, psychological safety, friendship, recognition, and respect. They also appreciate opportunities to learn and grow. People with socialized minds (those within stages one, two, or three of their psychological development) are not extremely loyal to a workplace. They may easily leave an organization for better benefits and/or higher pay.

The *self-authoring mind* is **independent**. Individuals in the fourth and fifth stages of their psychological development are driven by workplaces that give them autonomy, empowerment, and the opportunity to take initiative. They are ambitious, focused on achievement, and usually strive towards organizational leadership roles. Individuals with a self-authoring mind tend to view their work as a career. They are motivated and highly engaged by meaningful work, continuous evolvement, and growth. If these are unavailable in an organization, they will leave to search for purposeful work and development opportunities that will further their careers.

Finally, the *self-transforming mind* is an **interdependent** mind. People who have evolved to this stage of their psychological development think of their work as a calling or a mission. They are motivated by opportunities to satisfy their second growth needs and are highly engaged when they can make a difference in the world—in people's lives—and serve humanity. I must point out here that sometimes people are fortunate enough to have found their calling early on in life without necessarily going through all the stages of psychological development. A great example of such types of professions is doctors and nurses.

Based on all these theories, it is essential to note that industries and organizations must adapt their strategies for motivating their workforce and creating high engagement based on their audience and their employees' psychological development. For this to happen, leaders and managers must have deep, honest, and ongoing conversations to understand what motivates their employees. The more they know about their employees, the better they can motivate them. Furthermore, they may wish to take note of the ways an individual prefers to be appreciated and recognized for extraordinary work.

Suppose your organization predominantly employs people to do low-complexity work. In that case, it is probable that these employees are operating with their socialized minds. Thus, your company's motivational strategy must, at a minimum, satisfy their basic needs: remuneration and benefits, connections, and psychological safety. Similarly, companies that employ knowledge workers and/or highly skilled talents should consider what motivates people operating with self-authoring minds and self-transforming minds.

Many companies employ a mixture of the three types of minds. Motivation strategies must therefore be tailored accordingly.

Here is something else worth mentioning. Drastic changes in life circumstances may alter an employee's psychological development, hence altering what motivates them. Examples include the need for significantly larger remuneration (as in my case with the townhouse) or reduced working hours and responsibilities due to a family emergency (like taking care of a sick relative). Once these circumstances are resolved, the individual usually returns to their previous level. I began this chapter with a story about my real estate investment and the immediate need for a higher salary. I can assure you that it changed my motivations at work swiftly, and I found myself operating from a socialized mind. Before that, I was transitioning from a self-authoring mind to a self-transforming one.

I invite you to think about what your employees are going through—about the employee who recently had a child, or the individual whose family member is severely injured, or the talent who recently completed a Ph.D. and wants a more challenging role. What factors do you think will motivate them and drive a stellar performance from your team? What can you do about it? But don't just think about it and then assume you are right. What's crucial here is to have candid conversations with team members and to know them well.

PROUD OF YOUR WORK, PROUD OF YOUR COMPANY

This section will focus on workplace pride and how this can affect engagement and drive performance. Throughout my career, I have been extremely proud of many workplaces. Unfortunately, there were years when the reputation of one of these workplaces as an employer could have been better (as is the case with many organizations). Employee turnover was at 46% per annum. Some policies were not people-centric, and the long working hours the industry is infamous for did little for our work–life balance. Nevertheless, I was proud of my work because I was certain it positively impacted others and I believed I was uniquely qualified to do what I did. I went above and beyond, completing every job perfectly, often crying with admiration for what my team and I accomplished!

Pride. A largely unexplored driver of performance. How can we build more of it?

I love interweaving theory and scientific proof to complement my rich work experience. As such, this next section is inspired by a study commissioned by WorkProud and carried out by Dr. Rick Garlick and Dr. Bob Nelson, who are colossal talents in the field of employee experience, workplace culture, motivation, rewards, and recognition. One of the major drivers in The Great Place to Work model is workplace pride, and this prominent international workplace certification primarily focuses on cultivating pride and trust at work.

Pride, in relation to work, can be split into two concepts. First, having pride in your work: a driver of employee engagement, being present, job satisfaction, and going the extra mile. Second, being proud of your company: a driver of employee advocacy, retention, and business profitability. If you can successfully influence these two factors, you have achieved one of the main ingredients in the secret recipe for employee motivation, high morale, and discretionary effort.

On the other hand, someone with extreme pride in their work may become disgruntled if they cannot be equally proud of their workplace. Sadly, I have been in that position. I worked in a company that dragged out redundancies for over a month and a half with very little communication from the leadership team. People suddenly disappeared from one day to the next. It felt a little like *Squid Game*, the Korean drama series on Netflix. One day, I came into work and asked a colleague, "Where is Jack?" His response was quite sad. He said, "He isn't here, and I don't know who to ask."

Workplaces with toxic cultures are everywhere, and anyone at any level can cause this toxicity. However, people in a position of power usually carry the biggest responsibility for nurturing a psychologically safe environment. They must be willing to act against those who contribute to workplace toxicity, even if they hold high-ranking positions. My hope is that everyone who reads this book will be instrumental in building the right kind of culture, where individual and workplace pride are everyday things.

The culture of the organization drives company pride. The diagram below demonstrates the four influences of workplace pride, as shared in the WorkProud study.

PROUD OF YOUR WORK || PROUD OF YOUR COMPANY

INTENSIVE DRIVE

This factor speaks to the internal motivation that drives pride due to the feeling that one's work is important, as well as the strong drive the individual holds to making sure the "job is well-done."

RECOGNITION

Pride that comes from informal or formal recognition from leaders, managers, or peers acknowledging an employee's behavior, work, or business results which support the organization's business goals.

EXTERNAL VALIDATION

External validation occurs when friends, relatives, and cohorts outside the company remark on the prestige associated with the job and the company.

CULTURE

The pride people experience when they feel that their company's mission and values are personally meaningful, business is conducted ethically, leaders care about their employees and that companies are good corporate citizens.

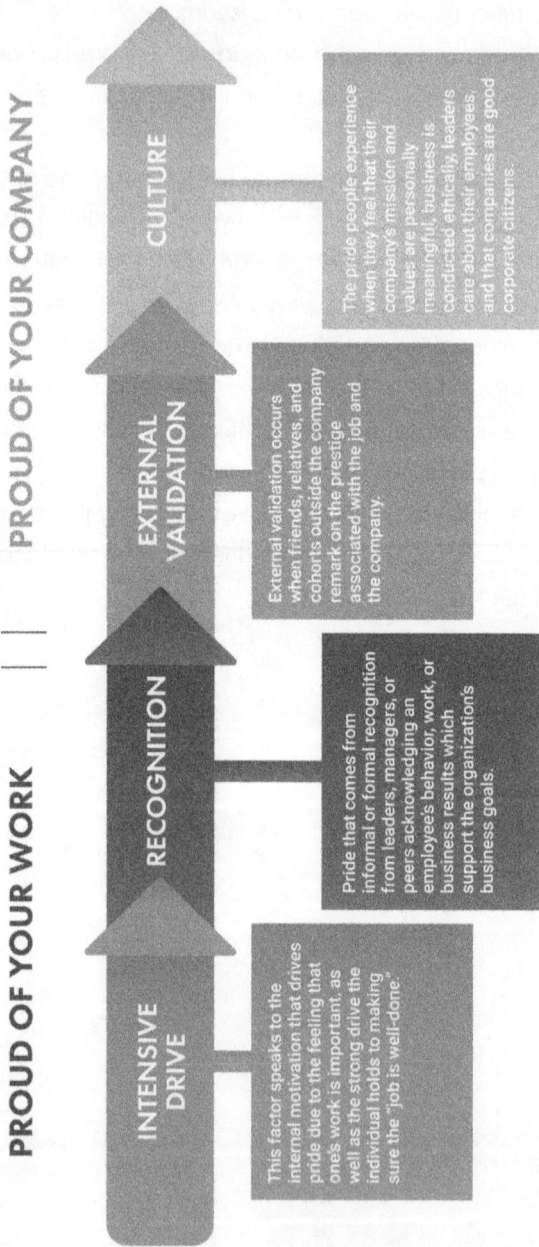

FIGURE 11. THE FOUR INFLUENCES OF WORKPLACE PRIDE

This book discusses all four of these influences. Two of them—intrinsic drive and recognition—are discussed in this very chapter. Individuals with great employee experiences are generally proud of their work and company. Leaders who successfully build workplaces that facilitate a unified culture of pride benefit from improved team collaboration and high employee engagement rates.

How do you build a culture where employees experience pride regularly? Figure 11 shows that consistent and high-quality rewards and recognition across all organizational levels are critical drivers of pride. An overall conclusion made in the study suggests that pride is one of the most significant influences on the overall employee experience, so let's look at some fundamentals of rewards and recognition next.

APPRECIATION, RECOGNITION, AND REWARDS

Many of us have seen how excited parents get when their newborn does something amazing, whether learning how to walk, sharing fruit with their friend, blowing a kiss, or putting their toys away. And what does the parent do? They praise, clap, and cheer as a sign of encouragement. This is positive reinforcement, and it usually comes instinctually to parents. Most parents intuitively return to basics, to their roots and instincts, because increasing the desired behavior happens by recognizing, applauding, and rewarding it. The desired behavior will then tend to be repeated.

Positive reinforcement is one of the most validated principles in psychology, made famous by psychologist B. F. Skinner. It also works exceptionally well in management and leadership. In recent years, the role of an effective leader has metamorphosed from an authoritative, controlling boss to a partner and collaborator who empowers, trusts, and coaches for success; someone who fosters a workplace culture of motivation, encouragement, appreciation, recognition, and rewards. You may argue that certain industries, even societies, still warrant a despotic method of management where recognition has no place. We will have to agree to disagree on this, as working with thousands of people from all over the globe has taught me otherwise. Throughout the years, I have been invited to judge multiple international industry awards based on employee happiness, customer experience, workplace culture, and employee engagement. The quality of human resources practices and their evolution continues to raise the bar. I have seen that the participating companies have one thing in common: the endless thirst to improve their workplace culture and to include appreciation, celebration, recognition, and rewards in their employee experience strategy.

Just like our parents may have given us support, love, and encouragement, we as managers and leaders must endorse and support the organization's recognition and rewards programs to empower our teams, reinforce desired behaviors, and improve people's performance in the work environment. The Apple TV series *Ted Lasso* perfectly illustrates this type of leadership. I am sure those who have seen the series will agree. Ted Lasso is a fictional coach who leads his team to personal and professional success through the power of his leadership style. He is a true gem. The series is an ideal example of how rewards, recognition, good communication, and empathy can change a failing culture into a thriving one.

Effective recognition programs drive individual and team performance, ultimately leading to organizational success. These programs incentivize and acknowledge desired behaviors that align with the company's mission, vision, core values, employee value proposition, strategic objectives, annual and long-term goals, and KPIs. With a positive approach toward achieving these objectives, businesses can succeed.

Before we go on, I'd like to unpack some terminology:

Appreciation: Usually verbal, this is about acknowledging someone's worth (while recognition is about appreciating their actions). In simple terms, appreciation is about who they are, and recognition is for what they do. Appreciation is a type of recognition that is not based on achieving a particular goal. When being appreciated, someone is made to feel valued.

Recognition: This could be verbal or written, private or public. Recognition is about acknowledging a specific task or goal the person has completed. It is essential that the recipient feels both recognized *and* appreciated simultaneously.

Reward: A tangible item of value, such as a certificate, a special meal, a trophy, or a cash prize—something special for going above and beyond. Once the desired behavior is exhibited and the results are achieved, the person is rewarded. Usually, recognition and rewards go hand in hand.

Incentive: This is typically a signing bonus for new employees; it also includes tips/gratuities where applicable, a service charge, a sales target, or a cash prize for the employee of the month. It is usually a monetary encouragement to achieve a specific goal or perform to a specific standard.

Celebration: A special event to celebrate and recognize an achievement or a meaningful milestone.

Total Rewards/Remuneration: The total monetary and non-monetary benefits that an individual (and their family) receives when working in an organization. This can include salary, medical and life insurance, travel/transportation allowance, housing allowance, educational allowance, various types of paid leave, children/spouse allowances, employee discounts, and company shares. It can also include benefits such as tips, an annual performance-based bonus, workplace tenure award, incentives, workplace experience, psychological safety, training, growth, and promotions.

It is critical that all these strategies work together to create the picture of total rewards.

When I mention rewards and recognition throughout this chapter, I am not referring to total renumeration. I am referring to purposefully celebrating occasions that matter in people's lives, appreciating them for their outstanding performance, and rewarding them for going above and beyond.

Implementing employee recognition for outstanding performance as part of the company culture has numerous proven benefits, such as increased trust, morale, happiness, productivity, competitiveness, revenue, and profit. It also leads to decreased stress, absenteeism, employee turnover, and related attrition costs. There is a big difference between paying people to come to work and motivating them to come to the office and do their best. This chapter aims to outline this.

When creating or revising a rewards and recognition (R&R) strategy, it's crucial to consider the company's culture, assess the health of a company's recognition climate, and help define what will and will not work. Determine what aligns with the culture and what does not, both now and in the future. Over the years, I have created many programs that prioritize appreciation, recognition, and rewards. I can confidently say that a well-thought-out, multipronged R&R strategy that includes organizational, team, and individual recognition can radically change the company culture and create a sustainable and thriving bottom line. Equally important is training managers and leaders on the *art* of meaningful and genuine recognition.

Organizations may cite a shortage of financial resources and inadequate budget as justifications for not developing an R&R strategy. The expenses associated with employee turnover are much greater than establishing a workplace culture where individuals feel valued and incentivized to exceed expectations. Although best-case practice suggests spending an average of $150–350 per person per year, R&R doesn't necessarily involve money and gifts. Consistent feedback from leaders can aid in personal growth and development, ultimately leading to a more productive and successful team.

EMBEDDING RECOGNITION IN THE CORPORATE CULTURE

A culture of recognition should be an integral part of the organization's strategy. One way to ensure this happens is by forming recognition KPIs linked to achieving company goals. Recognition must also be SMART:

Specific, Meaningful, Accurate/Sincere, Rewarding, and Timely.

Managers and leaders must be evaluated on their efforts to create and provide SMART recognition goals. Oh, and let's not forget to recognize the recognizers!

Another way to ensure recognition becomes part of the culture is to make recognition events impressive, fun, creative, and exciting. There are a variety of ways to make this happen on a budget. Effective communication and employee marketing are also crucial for such programs' success, as are constant progress tracking, assessment, and other feedback mechanisms. If a program stops functioning, it's time to re-evaluate, review, and update it.

To maintain a consistently positive culture, it is imperative to connect rewards and recognition with HR systems, employer branding, new-hire selection, recruiting, company orientation, onboarding, training and development, and performance appraisals. How well a leader fosters an environment of SMART recognition can also be one criterion for promotion.

I have outlined some tried-and-tested celebration, recognition, and rewards events in the following chart. For R&R to become part of corporate culture, as many people as possible must be involved in giving and receiving it daily. The examples below are provided to help and inspire your own workplace strategies. Remember, for them to work, they must all align with each other and the organization.

Naturally, a strategy encompassing all or most of these factors cannot be achieved overnight. It is imperative that the leadership and management team fully support and invest in the program and genuinely intend to participate. For long-term sustainability of the strategy, it is crucial to establish precise and measurable guidelines and criteria, prioritize transparency, and create equal opportunities for everyone to partake.

Table 3. The Celebration Guidelines Chart

Recognition Type	Timing and frequency	Setting and context	Recognition Provider	Examples of Rewards
Organizational company recognition for employee of the month, quarter, and year	Set up as an official part of the engagement calendar, this recognition may be monthly, quarterly, or yearly, as per the policy of the program. It must be credible, honest, and equitable, and people must be able to rely on it happening on time, every time. Nomination criteria must be clear, transparent, and equitable. Always look at keeping things fresh and relevant, changing aspects of the program based on relevant feedback, and having as many winners as the budget permits.	Public recognition during a ceremony, announcements on the company intranet, a wall of fame, company newsletter, noticeboards, etc. Be aware that people may be shy and may feel that public recognition is a negative consequence, so recognize them in a more private way.	Senior leadership may give out the awards in a public ceremony; the choice of whom to recognize and reward could come from the direct supervisor or manager of the individual. Recognition should be used as a strategic leadership tool. Overall, the nominators should be in alignment when recognizing individuals and teams, and they should be guided by behaviors aligned with organizational goals.	Customized trophies, certificates, company-wide announcements, ceremonies, special public wall-of-fame acknowledgment, merchandise, cash, loyalty points to be collected, paid vacations, special lunch/dinner celebrations, growth and development opportunities, job shadowing. Companies that have a hybrid workforce or operate on a global level may think about creating online virtual celebrations and sending gift items to teams in different countries.

Recognition Type	Timing and frequency	Setting and context	Recognition Provider	Examples of Rewards
Formal long-service awards	The cycle would be annual, but the number of years celebrated in terms of long service or company loyalty may be 3, 5, 7, 10, 15, or as per the company's program. Completion of the probation period as well as one year in the company can also be celebrated at a different event. Consider renewing your program if it is old and irrelevant. Be sure to obtain feedback from different people and departments.	Public recognition with a beautiful event, so that those recognized will feel valued and appreciated. Announcements on the company intranet or a recognition platform, wall of fame.	As this is organizational recognition and it has a broader and more ongoing impact, senior leadership must be involved.	In addition to a celebratory event and extra days off, loyal employees may receive opportunities for growth through extra learning and development opportunities or mentorship/coaching as a recognition of their commitment to the company. Companies that have a hybrid working force or operate on a global level may think about creating online virtual celebrations and sending gift items to teams in different countries.

Recognition Type	Timing and frequency	Setting and context	Recognition Provider	Examples of Rewards
Great Place to Work certification celebration (for high engagement survey scores)	This will be a company-wide celebration and may highlight certain departments that have achieved exemplary scores or have demonstrated growth by following their improvement action plans. The frequency will be yearly, or as often as company-wide surveys are carried out.	Public recognition is required here because rewarding what matters to the company sets the tone for all departments to follow. If a particular department has achieved a high score in a certain dimension of the engagement survey, they may showcase their achievements as a best-case practice for others to follow or be inspired by.	Senior leadership together with the HR team; possibly the corporate office.	Big town-hall meeting; large party to celebrate the achievements. Companies that have a hybrid workforce or operate on a global level may think about creating online virtual celebrations and sending gift items to the teams in different countries.

Recognition Type	Timing and frequency	Setting and context	Recognition Provider	Examples of Rewards
Cultural events (to celebrate national days and religious or historical holidays)	Companies may have an annual calendar of events that focus on diversity and inclusion, and these events will be celebrated as per a calendar, which should be communicated to the organization at the beginning of each year.	This type of event may cater to a particular nationality or group of people, and they may wish to celebrate it amongst themselves. However, for the sake of inclusivity and awareness, the celebration of national days, religious holidays, and major historical days should include everyone who wishes to attend. This creates social connections and better communication.	These events would typically be organized by the HR team or a committee for social wellbeing; the people celebrating a particular holiday could lead the celebrations with the assistance of their managers, the HR team, and the social committee.	Normally these types of events would have traditional food and beverages, as well as cultural performances such as a dance or ceremony as per historical tradition, etc. During religious celebrations, the HR team may give an appropriate gift to everyone in the organization to raise awareness and take the opportunity to appreciate all employees.

These celebrations can also be done virtually if required. |

Recognition Type	Timing and frequency	Setting and context	Recognition Provider	Examples of Rewards
Non-contingent awards (such as annual staff party, family picnic, employee appreciation week, thank you festival)	This type of celebration is created for everyone in the company as a way for leadership to reward and recognize the entire organization for a successful year or the completion of a major project, or as a way to encourage and improve social connections. The event can also be a large team-building activity, a retreat, or even a week-long festivity. This is one way of embedding recognition in the corporate culture.	This public recognition may involve the families of employees as a way of encouraging pride among employees; it's also a fabulous approach to employer branding.	The HR team would organize these events in collaboration with managers, leaders, and the social wellbeing committee; it could also involve volunteers.	Customized trophies for specific categories of awards, certificates, company-wide announcements, ceremonies, intranet communication, town halls, merchandise, cash, loyalty points to be collected, raffle draws, etc. Companies that have a hybrid workforce or operate on a global level may think about creating online virtual celebrations and sending gift items to teams in different countries.

Recognition Type	Timing and frequency	Setting and context	Recognition Provider	Examples of Rewards
Departmental recognition (for surpassing a target, an act of bravery or kindness, innovation)	Daily, weekly, monthly, and quarterly celebrations. Often, the core values and the mission and vision of the company will impact what will be celebrated; this will also be led by the company culture. So, if Corporate Social Responsibility (CSR) is big on the agenda, relevant accomplished milestones should be celebrated.	This could be done during a team or town-hall meeting. It could also be announced through the company communication app or noticeboards, depending on the magnitude of the accomplishment. If it's an individual accomplishment and they prefer private recognition, this should be respected.	Someone who has a great relationship with the person being recognized. If it's a team celebration, then senior leadership can also get involved.	A personal letter from the CEO to the awardee, cash prize for an act of bravery, development opportunities, merchandise, and company touchpoints could also be awarded to a wider team. Special recognition vacation for something major achieved. If it's a company-driven program, the rewards and recognition for exceeding a target should be pre-defined and used as motivation. There should be clear targets and incentives if the goals are attained.

Recognition Type	Timing and frequency	Setting and context	Recognition Provider	Examples of Rewards
Departmental trainer awards	If Learning and Development is a big part of an organization, departments may have colleagues in charge of training their employees; they should be rewarded for this extra task. This is the type of celebration that encourages a culture of growth, and it should be done quarterly. There must be targets for each department, to ensure fair and equitable recognition.	This celebration would normally be organized privately between the departmental trainers and the leaders. It is not necessary to have a company-wide celebration.	The HR team would oversee this type of recognition ceremony, as they are the custodians of a culture of growth and development.	A visible and accessible hall-of-fame wall with the top achievers in terms of training their teams (measured in hours per month, effectiveness of training, or desired outcomes); it could also be an award for the person who achieved the highest number of training hours in the entire department or company. The award could be something related to education, such as sponsorship of an external course or a book voucher.

Recognition Type	Timing and frequency	Setting and context	Recognition Provider	Examples of Rewards
Recruitment referral program	This kind of program usually awards employees for referring someone outside of the company for an organizational vacancy. If the new joiner is successful, then the employee gets a pre-agreed sum of money. This saves recruitment time or agency fees. If the program works well, it could indicate that the employee brand is strong and that individuals are proud of their workplace and are happy to refer others to work there.	As this is a monetary transaction, it should occur privately through the bank account of the employee.	Led by the HR and/or recruitment team.	Monetary award to the person who referred someone suitable for a company vacancy.

Recognition Type	Timing and frequency	Setting and context	Recognition Provider	Examples of Rewards
Outstanding day-to-day performance	Usually, this should occur immediately or soon after the behavior has been witnessed.	Public or private. Could occur on the company recognition platform or on the intranet via an e-badge or an e-card.	Department head, leader, manager, supervisor; someone that the person being recognized respects and holds in high regard.	Handwritten thank-you card, support and more involvement in a project, more autonomy, or authority (such as 'acting manager' for a period of time, if this is what motivates them). Allow people to select from a few reward options. Recognition vacation for multiple nominations.

Recognition Type	Timing and frequency	Setting and context	Recognition Provider	Examples of Rewards
Peer-to-peer recognition	This type of award can be given from any level to any level. If there is no official awards ceremony, employees can nominate each other at any time, and their nominations could be read/given out on a weekly basis. If there is an official peer-to-peer ceremony, the nominations can be communicated as per the chosen timeframe.	Mostly public, but if there are individuals who prefer private recognition, their recognition can be given from one person to another without the presence of others. Could occur on the company recognition platform or on the intranet via an e-badge or an e-card.	Any individual at any level in the organization.	Vouchers, certificates, pins; usually these awards wouldn't be of very high value. Allow people to select from a few reward options; give recognition leave for multiple nominations. Companies that have a hybrid workforce or operate on a global level may create online virtual recognition and send gift items to deserving individuals.

Recognition Type	Timing and frequency	Setting and context	Recognition Provider	Examples of Rewards
Informal or on-the-spot recognition	Usually, this should occur immediately or soon after the behavior/ performance has been witnessed.	Public or private. Could occur on the company recognition platform or on the intranet via an e-badge or an e-card.	Any individual at any level in the organization, but it's usually top to bottom.	Vouchers, certificates, pins; usually these awards wouldn't be of very high value. Part of the reward could be participation in a monthly raffle draw for something more substantial. Allow people to select from a few reward options.
Direct recognition (from customers directly, or from the company as a result of great customer care)	This is double recognition in some cases, especially if the company also rewards you for something that the customer has already appreciated. This type of award works well in any industry that prioritizes customer satisfaction and encourages employees to put the customer first.	Publicly at a town-hall meeting or in a departmental briefing setting; if the person being recognized prefers private recognition, this should be respected.	This would usually come from the supervisors or the managers. If the person being recognized is at a high level, the reward could come from the CEO. The higher the level of the person giving the award, the more weight it usually carries.	This can be enabled through company feedback forms, surveys, 'have your say' cards, etc. Any mechanism where customers could leave a written or verbal comment about an employee can be used. Allow people to select from a few reward options.

Recognition Type	Timing and frequency	Setting and context	Recognition Provider	Examples of Rewards
Industry award/industry sports competition, etc. (team or individual)	This can be done whenever there is a victory to be celebrated; often, it is teamwork that has led to the company's success, so we must recognize the individuals' strengths that contributed to the overall win.	This would most often occur in a public setting.	Leadership or management.	Team-spirit wall, a video about the entire team's achievement, a mention in the company newsletter, mention on the intranet or at a town-hall meeting, etc. This could be monetary or non-monetary. For instance, if the team has won something sports-related, they could receive sports gear, outfits, or memberships to a gym with personal trainers. Allow people to select from a few reward options.

Recognition Type	Timing and frequency	Setting and context	Recognition Provider	Examples of Rewards
Moments that matter (birthdays, graduations, graduation of a child, marriage, birth of a child, acknowledging major illnesses or death of a loved one)	These special moments may be celebrated within departments on a case-by-case basis. The timing and frequency will be as often as necessary, most probably on a weekly or monthly basis depending on the size of the department.	This would most often occur in a public setting, especially birthdays and joyful moments. Could occur on the company recognition platform or on the intranet. Significant moments such as hospitalization or bereavement will warrant private acknowledgment, care, and compassion. Companies that have a hybrid workforce or operate on a global level may think about creating online virtual celebrations and sending gift items to teams in different countries.	The HR team could get involved and reward employees for achieving certain milestones in their private life too, as this demonstrates that the company cares about the moments that matter to you. This recognition could also be done within the department. In terms of hospitalization, illness, or sad news, the HR team and head of department will need to be involved with support and compassion.	For joyful moments, departments can organize cakes, birthday celebrations, or surprise departmental parties. I used to work in an organization that gave out brand new laptops to the children of employees who graduated high school! Illness or bereavement are indeed moments that matter in an employee's life, so company policies around compassionate leave and monetary support should be established alongside grief counselling and resilience training.

Recognition Type	Timing and frequency	Setting and context	Recognition Provider	Examples of Rewards
Annual bonus, service charge, etc.	This is usually calculated based on individual, departmental, and company performance.	As this is a monetary transaction, it will occur privately through the bank account of the employee.	Leadership.	An individual thank-you letter from the CEO.
Signing bonus incentive (for a new joiner)	As a sign of appreciation for a new joiner choosing a particular company, the organization may wish to award a signing bonus for all new employees.	As this is a monetary transaction, it will occur privately through the bank account of the employee.	The onboarding/talent acquisition team.	An individual thank-you letter/video from the CEO can be sent to the new joiner; the signing bonus can be paid with their first salary.
Miscellaneous	As frequently as necessary.	Private or public, depending on the situation.	Appreciation, celebration, rewards, and recognition should be multi-directional in order for a culture of recognition to thrive.	Special considerations, assignments, projects, promotions, succession planning, secondments, special mentions, exceptions to the general rule as per company discretion.

THE DARK SIDE OF RECOGNITION AND REWARDS

Positive reinforcement, such as R&R, is considered extrinsic motivation. Companies who wish to cultivate high-performing workplace cultures should learn that extrinsic motivation must go hand in hand with intrinsic (internal) motivation. This is why it is essential for individuals in managerial or leadership positions to understand what motivates a person intrinsically and encourage that as much as possible. Extrinsic motivation based on positive reinforcement is not enough for high performance in the long run. The individual must be intrinsically motivated, and their stage of psychological development must be understood and nurtured. Thus, workplaces must not rely solely on R&R but on understanding motivation concepts, driving them, and building a sense of workplace pride. Tailoring R&R to the needs of individuals is essential, as effective R&R can look very different from person to person.

THE RIPPLE EFFECT

In this chapter, I discussed improving performance by motivating employees, fostering a sense of workplace pride, showing appreciation, recognizing discretionary effort, and providing rewards.

As we saw, motivation can be either intrinsic or extrinsic. There are different levels of motivation, and a person's psychological journey plays a significant factor in what will motivate or demotivate them. When it comes to pride, there are two types: pride for personal achievements and pride for a company's accomplishments.

The latter can be driven by leadership and the HR team. In terms of recognition, this is more than just a gesture. It must be an authentic and heartfelt expression of appreciation. It's essential to deliver recognition in a way that connects with the recipient and makes them feel valued by the company. When rewards and recognition are given with sincerity, this can profoundly impact people's sense of worth and belonging. It makes individuals feel they truly matter.

Throughout this chapter, I discussed the powerful effects of genuine appreciation, meaningful rewards, recognition, and driving a sense of pride and motivation. These impactful elements can bring about positive business outcomes, enhance customer experiences, and uplift the individuals involved. But let's take this a step further. The importance of the topics covered in this chapter lies in the pursuit of doing what is morally right. As parents, it comes naturally to us; as humans, it's what we crave.

This chapter started with a quote from the Barrett Values Centre:

> *"The reason that leaders are interested in what motivates employees is that motivation leads to commitment, commitment leads to engagement, and engagement leads to high performance."*

I'd like to continue in the spirit of this quotation and say that unwavering commitment, engagement, and exceptional accomplishments lead to better social engagement and ultimately contribute to the growth of stronger communities, neighborhoods, and societies.

Organizations that foster a culture focused on appreciating and motivating employees can have an impact beyond just the workplace. Such cultures can shape individuals' conduct, both professionally and personally. By fostering ethical practices, businesses can positively impact the local community. This impact can be seen in how people treat their loved ones and appreciate their actions. A company's culture can extend far beyond its walls, and it is up to businesses to take responsibility for their impact on society.

Equally important is addressing the holistic wellbeing of the organization. This will be the topic of the next chapter.

CHALLENGE ACCEPTED: PUTTING *REWARDS AND RECOGNITION* INTO ACTION

Here are some strategic options you can contemplate after reading this chapter. These suggested activities will help improve your organization's motivation, pride, and rewards and recognition.

1. Play *Why I Appreciate You*

Task: Each team member writes down two colleagues' names on a card. On one side, they describe why they appreciate one colleague personally (kindness, humor, etc.). On the other side, they explain why they appreciate one colleague professionally (expertise, support, etc.).

Challenge: Highlight specific instances. Focus on genuine impact and positive traits.

Activity: Shuffle the cards and anonymously distribute them. Allow individuals to read their appreciation messages aloud, fostering connection and recognition.

2. Gratitude Graffiti

Task: Provide colorful sticky notes and markers in a central location. Encourage team members to leave positive messages, quotes, or words of encouragement anonymously.

Challenge: Spread kindness and inspiration throughout the work-space. Use visual prompts and humor to spark joy and connection.

Activity: Monitor the Gratitude Graffiti wall and periodically share noteworthy messages anonymously. Encourage positive vibes throughout the month.

3. Cultivate Ambassadors of Innovation

Task: Identify and empower a group of passionate employees to drive innovation and challenge the status quo. Provide them with dedicated resources, training, and access to leadership.

Challenge: Look for individuals with diverse perspectives, creativity, and a willingness to push boundaries. Encourage them to experiment with new technologies, processes, and business models.

Activity: Establish an Innovation Lab for these ambassadors to collaborate, prototype, and present their ideas. Provide opportunities for them to share their progress with management and the wider team.

CHAPTER 11

EMPLOYEES WANT WELLBEING FROM THEIR JOBS, AND THEY MAY RESIGN TO FIND IT

"What if the next global crisis is a mental health pandemic?"

This question was posed some time ago by the Chairman and CEO of Gallup, Jim Clifton, in the editorial note of Gallup's *State of the Global Workplace 2021 Report*. The annual report features findings from the world's largest ongoing study of the employee experience.

According to the latest report, the world has recovered from the worst of the pandemic, and engagement levels have risen, but stress remains at an all-time high, staying true to the trend that began nearly a decade ago. This stress is a combination of factors such as work, family, health, finances, security, and others. Gallup's analysis concludes that employees report significantly lower stress in their lives when they are engaged at work.

In this chapter, I will review the state of workplaces globally by looking at data from reputable companies specializing in employee-related research. The aim is to give you a holistic understanding of what wellbeing is and how leaders and managers have a responsibility in the lives of their employees and their families. You will also come out with a clear picture of an authentic wellbeing strategy and how you can integrate it into your company culture. Employee wellbeing is vital to employee engagement and integral to a positive employee experience.

Let's look at what is happening in the world of employee wellbeing.

As one of the world's leading research organizations, Gallup specializes in gathering data from millions of people globally and consulting on employee engagement and wellbeing. During the COVID-19 pandemic, its findings were alarming.

Globally, employee engagement decreased by 2% (from 22% in 2019 to 20% in 2020). But it's not this decrease that distresses me. It is the actual percentage of engaged workers. Only 20% of employees globally are engaged at work! This means that an enormous chunk (80%) of the global population is disengaged. In both the 2020 and the 2023 report, participants reported record-high negative emotions such as stress (44%), anger (21%), worry, and sadness. Additionally, Gallup found that approximately seven in ten employees are struggling instead of thriving in their lives. Suffering destroys the human spirit. It destroys lives. This has an adverse effect on productivity, innovation, and jobs.

Looking at these numbers, you might immediately think that 2020 was a one-off year and these record levels resulted from COVID-19. The truth is, as the concerning numbers tell us, that these problems existed pre-COVID-19.

The following graph demonstrates global engagement scores since the first survey in 2009. Two things are worth noting. Engagement scores are on the rise. Also, companies demonstrating best-case practices regarding employee engagement have very healthy scores compared to other organizations.

Employee Engagement Trends

% Engaged

● Best-practice organizations   ● Global

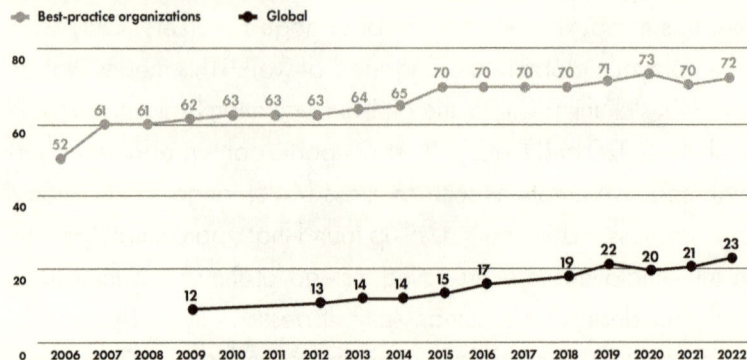

FIGURE 12. EMPLOYEE ENGAGEMENT TRENDS

What do these companies do? Well, many talented workers constantly leave their workplaces and join organizations that show genuine concern and care for the wellbeing of their employees.

Thus, if companies don't implement broad-scale intervention for engagement and wellbeing, employee mental health could suffer. Organizational leaders can reverse the negatively spiraling trend by prioritizing employee wellbeing. In the latest Gallup report, respondents were asked: *What would you change about your workplace to make it better?* Eighty-five percent of the responses offered by quiet quitters were related to engagement or culture, pay and benefits, or wellbeing and work–life balance. HR, management, and leadership can resolve these issues.

AND THAT'S NOT ALL ...

According to Microsoft's 2021 Work Trend Index, which surveyed approximately 30,000 people in thirty-one countries and analyzed trillions of productivity and labor signals across Microsoft 365 and LinkedIn, "high productivity is masking an exhausted workforce." One in five of the self-assessed respondents claim that their employer doesn't care about their work–life balance. Fifty-four percent feel "overwhelmed," and 39% feel "exhausted." This may be because digital intensity (the average number of virtual meetings and chats) employees are expected to participate in has increased tremendously.

Furthermore, Generation Z (born between 1997 and 2012) is at risk and will "need to be energized," according to the Work Trend Index. Respondents say they are "merely surviving." The youngest working generation of the respondents feel exhausted after work, struggle with balancing work with life, and find it difficult to feel engaged or excited about work. They also have a hard time with innovation during meetings.

But it isn't all doom and gloom. As employees navigate a new and frequently more stressful world, both at home and at work, they manage to connect with their co-workers in an unprecedented way. Increasingly, working virtually or in a hybrid environment has enabled colleagues to meet each other's pets and families, or see their CEOs doing yoga with their children in their living rooms! These types of interactions have fostered closeness and, in their own way, have brought people together. The 2021 Work Trend Index reports that, compared to 2020, 39% of respondents were more likely to "be their full authentic selves at work." People who interacted with each other more than they did previously experienced "stronger work relationships" and reported higher productivity and overall better wellbeing. And, as seen in the Gallup report from Figure 12, global employee engagement is on the increase.

Engagement and wellbeing go hand in hand. For this upward trend to continue, wellbeing must be integrated into the company's culture and be a visible part of the employer brand. Historically, workplaces view wellbeing as simply physical—or worse, they do not consider themselves responsible for enhancing and promoting wellbeing outside the generic remuneration, benefits, perks, and policies realm.

Well, guess what? Gallup asked employees what they look for most in an employer, and the data showed "an organization that cares about employees' wellbeing" in the top three criteria (together with diversity, equity, and inclusion). For millennials and Generation Z, it's the top workplace prerequisite!

According to the same source, workplace cultures with effectively integrated workplaces, wellbeing strategies, growth and promotion opportunities, and perceptions of fair pay have the highest employee retention rates.

WHAT CAN YOU DO ABOUT THIS?

You may already have a wellbeing strategy in place at work and may be looking to improve or revamp it, or you might need help figuring out where to start. In either case, together, we will go through a step-by-step process of putting together an inspiring, authentic strategy as part of your culture that will bring remarkable results and maximize the potential and wellbeing of every individual.

Before you begin strategizing, however, it is important to review select literature and define wellbeing. This will help you understand how the holistic elements of wellbeing can positively influence our workplaces and personal lives.

HEDONIC AND EUDAIMONIC WELLBEING

Scientists and psychologists Ryan and Deci defined two distinctive perspectives of wellbeing: *hedonic* and *eudaimonic*. From a hedonic perspective, wellbeing is defined in terms of feelings such as happiness and pleasure, life satisfaction, and positive affect (not feeling negativity); it is an aspect of wellbeing that can be empirically measured. This is generally referred to as emotional or *subjective wellbeing* (SWB), an expression coined by Ed Diener, a leading researcher in positive psychology.

The eudaimonic view of wellbeing recognizes the need for self-actualization and the desire to seek meaning and purpose in life. Also known as *psychological wellbeing* (PWB), eudaimonia is based on Aristotle's *Nicomachean Ethics,* focusing on living virtuously rather than just feeling good. It is defined by academics Ryff and Keys in terms of the six characteristics below. Most of these characteristics require individual retrospection and work. However, the last one can be explored in depth at work and beyond.

1. self-acceptance
2. personal growth
3. purpose (and meaning) in life
4. environmental mastery

5. autonomy
6. positive relations with others.

BUCKINGHAMSHIRE'S FIVE WAYS TO WELLBEING

Earlier, I mentioned Buckinghamshire's five ways to wellbeing (5WTW). Developed by the Oxford Health NHS Foundation Trust and other specialists on behalf of Buckinghamshire's Country Council Public Health Team, 5WTW is grounded in research. Understanding and applying the five ways offers employees deeper insight into their wellbeing, allowing them to connect meaningfully and engage with something bigger than their individual selves. The five ways to wellbeing are:

1. connecting with people (socially, through work, etc.)
2. giving (being generous)
3. taking notice (being mindful)
4. learning (through formal or informal education)
5. being active (physically).

GALLUP'S FIVE ELEMENTS OF WELLBEING

Gallup also proposes five elements of wellbeing, which have been identified through years of research in partnership with leading economists, psychologists, and scientists. Juxtaposed with

Buckinghamshire's 5WTW, we find good synergy between the two:

1. career wellbeing (this has the biggest impact on positive outcomes and is the foundation for thriving in all five elements)
2. social wellbeing (having meaningful relationships in your life)
3. financial wellbeing
4. physical wellbeing (to which I will also add nutritional wellbeing)
5. community wellbeing.

BUT WHAT ABOUT MENTAL WELLBEING?

At this point, it is paramount to discuss mental health. Its importance has been highlighted more than ever in 2020 and 2021, as the COVID-19 pandemic created an unprecedented situation. Gallup's *State of the Global Workplace 2021 Report* findings show that 45% of individuals surveyed say their life has been affected "a lot" by the coronavirus. Only 32% are thriving. Similarly, 43% experienced stress, 41% experienced worry during a lot of the previous day, 25% experienced sadness, and 24% experienced anger. These numbers have increased by one or several points yearly since 2009.

Daily Negative Emotions, Among Employees

Did you experience the following feelings during A LOT OF THE DAY yesterday?
How about [worry, stress, anger, sadness]?

% Yes

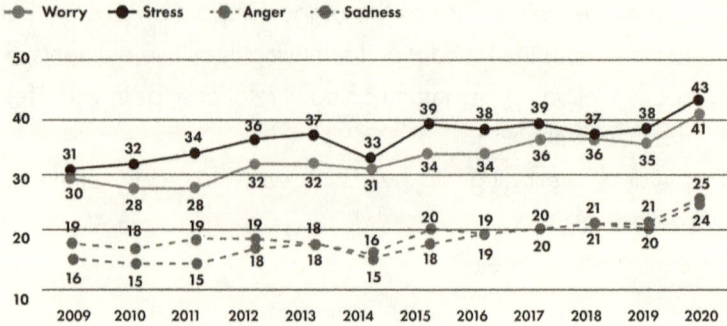

FIGURE 13. DAILY NEGATIVE EMPLOYEE EMOTIONS

According to various research, the elements of wellbeing suggested above deliver positive business and personal outcomes, decrease stress, increase happiness, increase resilience and adaptability, help improve job performance, and reduce employee turnover. Employee wellbeing plays a central role in the employee journey, and employees with good holistic wellbeing will be in a powerful position to deliver superior, world-class customer experiences.

THE CONCEPT OF FLOW

Coined by Mihaly Csíkszentmihályi, one of the most prominent figures in the field of positive psychology in the early 1990s, *flow* is a state where one is fully engaged in a task and is, figuratively speaking, flowing easily along a stream of creativity.

In his seminal work, *Flow: The Psychology of Optimal Experience*, Csíkszentmihályi proposed that people are happiest when experiencing flow. Positive psychologists associate flow with eudaimonia, as flow inherently results in growth by encouraging individuals to use their skills, thus leading to progressive development. Flow has to do with a heightened sense of motivation and extreme focus on a particular activity. According to Nakamura and Csíkszentmihályi, its characteristics include:

- intense and focused concentration on what one is doing at present
- merging of action and awareness
- loss of reflective self-consciousness
- a sense that one can control one's actions
- distortion of temporal experience
- experience of the activity as intrinsically rewarding, such that often the end goal is just an excuse for the process.

Conditions predisposing an individual to achieve flow include following or achieving one's immediate personal or professional goals, receiving instantaneous feedback on progress, and balancing between challenges and perceived skills. According to Csíkszentmihályi, being completely engaged in what you are doing at work is conducive to creating moments of flow; so are sports, art, and play.

Now that we have reviewed what the literature says about wellbeing, it is time to introduce some practical ways of applying various elements of wellbeing to workplace culture.

WELL CERTIFICATION

This section combines the wellbeing elements discussed earlier with additional ones and guides workplaces through a well-renowned certification process for meeting wellbeing standards.

WELL is a certification that applies all aspects of wellbeing to benefit people's health and work performance. For workplaces to become WELL certified, they must meet several criteria in a points system based on the following:

- the mind
- the community
- movement
- water
- air
- light
- thermal comfort
- nourishment
- sound
- materials.

This certification verifies that an organization has implemented evidence-backed, third-party-verified strategies to foster an inclusive environment where everyone feels welcome, seen, and heard. There is growing traction and support for this certification, and numerous countries worldwide have set ambitious goals to certify their organizations this decade. However, it's not just workplaces that are striving for certification. Residential buildings, malls, and entire communities are also pursuing it.

As described by Matthew Trowbridge, Chief Medical Officer, International WELL Building Institute:

"More than ever before, companies are being held to a higher standard for how they care for their employees and manage the downstream impacts of their products and services. IWBI applies the science in the WELL Building Standard to help organizations meet and exceed industry performance standards to become leaders in health."

Being WELL certified is not a simple process. The requirements and criteria are rigorous, and it may take several years and lots of changes to the workplaces before a company can attain the coveted platinum certification. There are also less stringent certifications, such as gold, silver, and bronze. Make no mistake, attaining these is no easy feat either.

The initial step toward corporate wellbeing is obtaining a health and safety rating from the WELL Building Institute, which forms the essential wellbeing foundation for any company when combined with a well-planned wellbeing strategy.

TRIED AND TESTED GUIDELINES AND RECOMMENDATIONS

My recommendations for companies aiming to create a holistic and inclusive work culture built with employee wellbeing at its heart is to put together a company-wide strategy and publish a yearly calendar that includes all elements for wellbeing. This can be reviewed on a quarterly basis to ensure business align-ment and relevance, and it should be marketed and communi-cated to the entire organization. Before embarking on a quest to incorporate wellbeing as part of a strategy and culture, be sure to take an initial measurement (usually through a wellbeing survey) of where the organization currently sits. Knowing what colleagues may be struggling with will help point leaders in the right direction.

People are more likely to support what they help create. Therefore, involving various stakeholders and people across departments, levels, nationalities, marital/education status, company tenure, cultures, and abilities in the strategy's devel-opment is crucial to its adoption and success. Be sure to mea-sure your success and failures after each initiative so you can consistently adapt, grow, and improve. This could occur via surveys, focus groups, and discussions. Remember: what gets measured gets managed.

I invite you to visit my website, www.beyond-employeeengagement.com, for a detailed tem-plate with practical and creative ways to incorporate wellbeing elements into your yearly holistic wellbeing plan and schedule.

WHAT ELSE CAN LEADERS DO BETTER?

Placing wellbeing at the heart of company culture can be achieved through a comprehensive and inclusive strategy. This can include initiatives such as events, activities, workshops, surveys, reviews, talent management, and other suggestions. The responsibility for implementing these initiatives can be shared among the engagement and experience team, departmental champions, volunteers, and external partners. What can leaders do that others may not be able to do?

Leaders can improve wellbeing in their workplaces by becoming better coaches and mentors and, if required, should speak up and get the right training. There are resources that can help build capabilities as a coach. Coaching is one of the most effective and critical skills for good leadership. When done right, coaching is paramount to employee progress and growth. According to Gallup, in the best organizations, when compared to their peers, employees who received strengths-based development showed lower turnover, higher engagement, and higher involvement in company-sponsored activities.

Connecting authentically and encouraging everyone to realign with the company mission, vision, and values is something else that can be revisited. Leaders can continue to build trust, hope, empathy, compassion, and stability. Building hope increases excitement about a better future. Leading with compassion and empathy means approaching matters with a genuine understanding of what is on others' minds. Instilling a sense of trust as a leader shows that a leader's words connect authentically to their actions. Encouraging a sense of stability at work creates consistency. This is all part of the wellbeing strategy.

THE *WHY* IN A NUTSHELL
(ONCE AGAIN)

Hopefully, you are better positioned to connect the dots between employee wellbeing and its impact on customer experience. An awesome wellbeing strategy must be defined, measured, and incorporated in the employee experience. We must work to create a better future and prioritize essential issues such as digital exhaustion. This includes reducing employee workload and promoting a culture where breaks are encouraged and respected.

Creating a targeted and meaningful wellbeing culture and teaching employees about their wellbeing fosters quality bonds. In addition, a sense of connectedness, happiness, mindfulness, and gratitude also encourages personal transformations. By encouraging employees to focus on their wellbeing, organizations can help them find meaningfulness in their jobs and make a career. This improves their lives, as well as their community.

In turn, this benefits the business. Weaving wellbeing into the organization's fabric helps improve the employee experience significantly, reducing employee turnover and the associated costs. By adopting wellbeing as part of their culture, businesses will experience reduced employee absenteeism and increased employee productivity, resulting in higher profits and memorable customer experiences.

This section has discussed the initial stages of the employee journey: attracting, hiring, onboarding, and engaging. Engagement is a continuous process that should be kept in mind throughout the entire employee experience, from start to finish and beyond. By recognizing the significance of internal communication, positive psychology, rewards and recognition, and wellbeing, we can foster engagement and enhance employees' experiences. The upcoming section concentrates on growth and performance, two stages that are equally important. Just like engagement, growth and performance should not be viewed as one-off events but rather as ongoing processes that require strategic planning and execution.

CHALLENGE ACCEPTED: PUTTING *WELLBEING* INTO ACTION

Below are several tasks that I encourage you to delve into once you finish reading this chapter.

1. Sleep Hackathon

Task: Organize a fun and informative workshop or competition focused on improving sleep habits. Invite a sleep expert to share tips and tricks.

Challenge: Go beyond basic sleep tips. Encourage creative solutions, peer support, and accountability for establishing healthier sleep routines. Consider incorporating sleep-tracking apps or wearable devices for data-driven approaches.

Activity: During the event, share resources, tips, and progress updates. After a set period, have teams present their sleep-hack solutions and celebrate successful improvements in sleep quality and overall wellbeing.

2. Personal Growth Book Club

Task: Form a book club focused on books related to personal growth, wellbeing, and achieving work–life balance. Choose books that resonate with your team's interests.

Challenge: Promote active engagement and reflection. Encourage members to share their takeaways, insights, and personal experiences related to the book's themes.

Activity: Organize regular discussions, guest speaker sessions, or workshops based on the chosen books. Consider inviting authors or experts to share their knowledge and perspectives on the book's themes.

3. Budgeting Bootcamp

Task: Organize a series of interactive workshops or online tutorials on practical budgeting skills. Cover topics like income tracking, expense categorization, saving strategies, and goal setting.

Challenge: Move beyond basic budgeting principles. Encourage participants to personalize their budgets based on individual needs, income, and spending habits. Provide tools and templates to facilitate budgeting implementation.

Activity: Hold 'budgeting clinics' where individuals can receive personalized feedback and guidance on their budgeting plans. Invite banking representatives or finance subject-matter experts and organize group discussions to share financial knowledge.

PART 4 Time to Shine

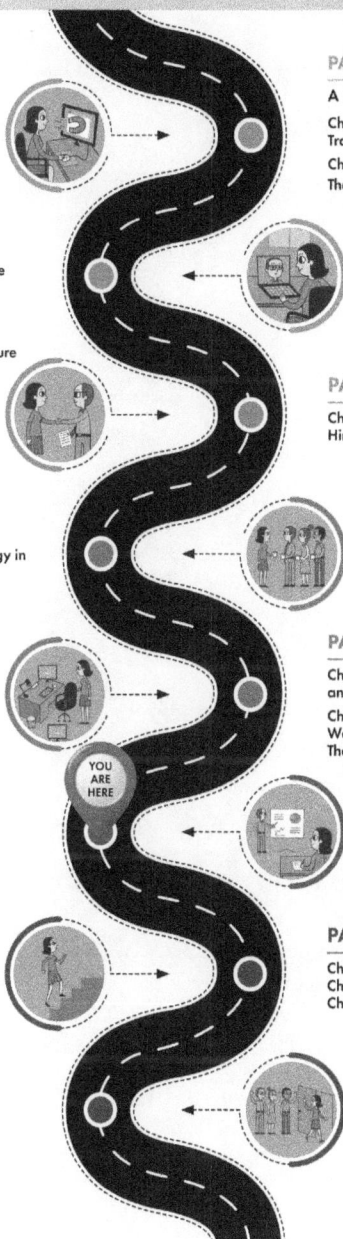

CHAPTER 12

LEARNING AND PERFORMANCE

"The only thing worse than training your employees and having them leave is not training them and having them stay."

—HENRY FORD, FOUNDER,
FORD MOTOR COMPANY

I am very passionate about continuous, purposeful learning that is intentionally put to good use. This includes learning at work and outside of work. Within the sphere of the employee experience, continuous learning, growth, and development form a massive chunk of the journey. If done well, they can positively affect the employee and the customer experience. We may begin to learn about (and from) an organization before joining it, but real growth and performance improvement usually occur while actually employed. This segment of the journey can last until the person exits an organization.

Most organizations are on board with the importance of workplace learning and development and the consequent advantage it gives them over their business competitors. Some go as far as developing a workplace culture deeply rooted in the tradition of growth and development. Tied intrinsically to performance and career growth, learning and development contribute to the company's and society's advancement. Workplaces are more responsible for providing continuous education to adults than any other educational institution.

As humans, we typically attend kindergarten and school until age eighteen (if we are fortunate enough to have been afforded formal education); this may be followed by another three to four years of university and perhaps another two years at a master's level. This would amount to approximately eighteen years of studying and implementing theory. The real test begins when we embark on a career journey. Usually, working life up to retirement continues for another forty years. This is twice as long as the amount of time we have spent at school, disregarding the enviable vacation schedules of most students.

Here is where accountable organizations take on responsibility as educators. This can be achieved through either classroom training with in-house facilitators or by bringing in external professionals. Due to budget constraints and prioritization, this training may focus on skills such as customer care, product upselling, leadership, and computer/software-related skills. This is so-called off-the-job training. As discussed in the chapter on wellbeing, exceptional organizations also recognize the importance of offering practical life-skills workshops such as sessions on wellbeing, mental health, resilience, financial education, and other topics that equip employees to be better human beings for themselves, their families, and their communities. Another way companies support the learning, growth, and development journey of their employees is by partnering with online training platforms such as LinkedIn Learning to deliver a plethora of ready-made modules.

On-the-job training, on the other hand, requires an individual to undergo training while simultaneously performing their duties, such as a housekeeper learning how to use a new power-washing tool, a new employee learning to operate the forklift, and an IT specialist learning about the latest software.

The theory of the 70/20/10 in learning and development suggests that learners absorb best by doing. Thus, 70% of their learning should be on-the-job stretch assignments and experiential learning. Another 20% should be peer coaching or mentoring. A strong performer may be encouraged to coach a high performer. This is advantageous to the strong performer, as it may lead to transformative learning. It is recommended that only 10% of employee development should consist of formal courses or classes focusing on skills that cannot be learned on the job.

Many organizations adopt a hybrid approach to learning. Some, however, don't prioritize it from a budgetary perspective. Regardless, these are all traditional strategies, and there is nothing wrong with tradition. But what if we adopted a different learning modality? Something more experiential, something more gamified?

This chapter on L&D and growth will be less conventional. I encourage you to look at different learning modalities. Learning cannot be forced. It must be embraced and sought by the individual. Numerous studies show that companies whose cultural mix includes training are better off regarding productivity, revenue, customer satisfaction, employee engagement, and retention. When I worked at one of the largest resorts in the Middle East, leaders often emphasized that working there for just one year was equivalent to attending university for three years! This is partly due to the intense learning culture, which was also reflected in the company values. So, besides obtaining a couple of pseudo-PhDs after thirteen years of working there, I also hold two genuine master's degrees from accredited professional bodies: an MBA in Telecoms and an MSc in Applied Positive Psychology.

One of my top five strengths assessed by the VIA Character Strengths Survey (the premier positive psychology tool for evaluating an individual's character strengths) is "love for learning." Another is "curiosity." As already mentioned in the chapter on employee engagement, for my second master's dissertation, I developed a fascinating prototype of an escape room with the primary focus of teaching Buckinghamshire's five ways to wellbeing (making meaningful connections with people, keeping active, giving, taking notice, and learning) through experiential gamified learning.

I am a big believer in edutainment. I've also researched and applied experiential and transformational learning to my work. Hence, the next part of this chapter will discuss the benefits of non-traditional education. Lastly, I offer some food for thought on performance appraisals and alternatives. Whatever mix of learning modalities organizations apply to their culture will result in a massive advantage over companies that do not invest in learning and growth.

So, let's get started!

A NON-TRADITIONAL APPROACH TO LEARNING

There is an intricately complex relationship between education and entertainment. This can be witnessed in educational leisure settings such as museums, art galleries, escape rooms, and wildlife and marine life centers. Individuals can gain knowledge, foster creativity, and experience personal transformation through this avenue. These benefits not only enhance their own lives but also positively impact their organizations and community.

Since the 1980s, research has demonstrated the benefits of marrying 'education' and 'entertainment' into 'edutainment.' Many scholars and authors, such as Packer and Ballantyne (2004), discuss the synergy between education and entertainment and how this is often conducive to a learning experience that transcends traditional classroom settings. Research also suggests that people increasingly seek fun and pleasurable leisure activities to counterbalance the mounting pressure in lifestyles, the increasing pace of life, and the diminishing work–life balance. According to Roberts (1997), entertainment-based settings, where play and fun are involved and exploration is encouraged, are optimal learning conditions because individuals are open and receptive.

Learning can be both challenging and intrinsically satisfying, and when a person feels motivated, learning occurs automatically and effortlessly (Hidi, 1990; Krapp, 1999). Individuals who seek educational experiences will find that edutainment settings enhance learning. This is one reason I was very excited while developing the wellbeing-themed escape room, as this was aimed at organizations who wished to add value to people's lives through edutainment in addition to the standard training modules on offer.

In research conducted by Packer and Ballantyne (2004), visitors of educational leisure settings agreed that information presented in an entertaining way helped them learn better, making education entertaining, discovery exciting, and learning an adventure. This was due to four features that define the educational leisure experience presented by Packer:

- discovery and fascination
- appeal to multiple senses
- appearance and effortlessness
- availability of choice.

LEARNING THEORIES: EXPERIENTIAL LEARNING

In addition to edutainment, it's important to point you toward experiential and transformative learning. Kolb (1984) posits that "learning is the process whereby knowledge is created through the transformation of experience."

Combining learning and actively experiencing something, especially with strong emotional outcomes, is best described as experiential learning (Fanning & Gaba, 2007). Experiential learning involves doing, thinking about, and assimilating the learning outcome.

Experiential learning theory (ELT) is built on the foundational works of prominent academicians from the twentieth century, such as Lewin, Dewey, Jung, and others who considered 'experience' to have a central role in human learning and development. In 1984, Kolb developed a holistic model based on research on the process of learning and published his learning styles model, from which he developed his learning style inventory. ELT is applicable in all sorts of settings, as learning from experience is not limited to formal classroom education. The holistic nature of learning means that it operates from an individual to a group, to an organizational and societal level.

Experiential learning (EL) is one cornerstone of organizational development efforts for many organizations worldwide. EL proposes the four-stage learning cycle in the following figure. The cycle allows the learner to go through the process of experiencing, reflecting, thinking, and acting.

In my dissertation for my Master's in Applied Positive Psychology, I proposed that this is also the case with learning in escape rooms.

In such puzzles, the gamemaster is the facilitator of the learning process, and together with the narrative of the game, they guide the participants through this four-step process. If you'd like to know more about my dissertation, you can get in touch with me through my website www.beyond-employeeengagement.com.

Effective learning is seen when a person progresses through this cycle. Concrete experiences are the basis for observations and reflections where a new situation is encountered or a reinterpretation of an existing experience is made. These reflections are assimilated and then taken through abstract concepts from which new actions (at work) can be undertaken. The actions can be tested and used as a guide in creating new experiences where the learner applies their new ideas at work, for instance. According to Kolb (1984), effective learning occurs when a person executes all four stages.

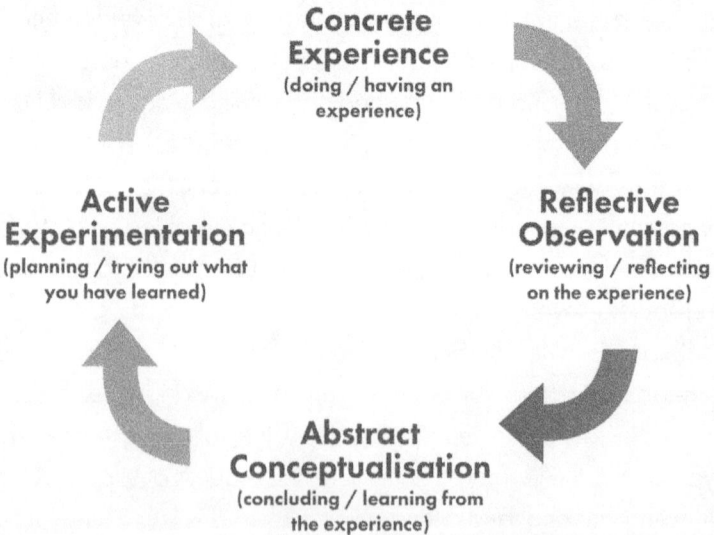

Concrete Experience
(doing / having an experience)

Reflective Observation
(reviewing / reflecting on the experience)

Abstract Conceptualisation
(concluding / learning from the experience)

Active Experimentation
(planning / trying out what you have learned)

FIGURE 14. LEWIN'S EXPERIENTIAL LEARNING MODEL

TRANSFORMATIVE LEARNING

For learning to be meaningful and beneficial, it must be transformative. For example, transformative learning should ideally help change a person's behavior, give them the strength to make decisions, or prepare them for a promotion. Learning is the process of making meaning out of life. This process is manifested by a journey of learning through experience; reflecting on the experience in relation to prior beliefs, education, culture, religion, upbringing, and exposure to the world; and potentially altering one's perception of these beliefs and making a change. This transformative learning process is guided by finding meaning (Mezirow, 1991). The cardinal goal of education is understanding, construing, validating, and reformulating the meaning of our experiences and being empowered to make our own interpretations through independent thinking. According to Mezirow, autonomous thinking is developed through transformative learning, and it aims to explain how our expectations and cultural traditions influence the meaning we derive from our experiences. If learners are to change their uncritically acquired childhood beliefs and general frames of reference and paradigms, they must critically reflect on their experiences. This may lead to a change in perspective, which leads to transformative learning. This type of breakthrough is often necessary when someone is promoted from manager to director, as their role and approach to the new designation changes significantly.

Central to Mezirow's theory are experience, critical reflection, and rational discourse. Transformation may happen when an individual engages with themselves and with others. Shared learning experiences may encourage co-learners to construct meaning through conversation or personal reflection. During transformative learning, the participant is analytical and emotional and uses conscious and unconscious thought.

In collective learning, such as in an escape room or a team-building exercise, transformation can happen through a combined change of the beliefs of all (or some) of the participants, and this can reach beyond an individual transformation and as far as an organizational and even a societal change.

Based on research by Taylor (1998), not all learners are able to go through transformative learning, and many adult learning situations are not conducive to transformative learning. The learner has a role to play in creating a favorable learning environment. Additionally, to foster a transformative learning environment, special attention must be paid to the part of the facilitator. An environment that rates highly on psychological safety is essential.

THE ROLE OF DEBRIEFING IN LEARNING

If learning occurs in a group, the learning experience is more meaningful if participants have been empowered to share thoughts, work, and interact as a team. Learning about others' perspectives and juxtaposing them with one's own is encouraged through customized debriefing sessions.

It is essential for educational experiences to conclude with a meaningfully structured debriefing session where all participants are brought together in a different environment and encouraged to engage in discussion based on their immersive game. A debriefing session helps the explorers process their experiences and consider how their learnings can be applied to real life to create long-lasting transformations.

In 1933, Dewey, an influential philosopher, psychologist, and educational theorist, proposed that "people do not learn from experience; they learn from reflecting on their experience." The function of reflection is to create meaning out of an experience. The more meaningful this experience, the more valuable it is.

Individuals are increasingly looking for memorable, experiential instances in learning and in other spheres of life, such as work. Experiential learning offers participants an immersive journey like no other. With this chapter, I aim to inspire organizations to think beyond traditional learning modalities and encourage their employees to participate in fun and transformative educational experiences that benefit both the individual and the organization. As a partner of one of the largest multinational logistics companies, I frequently organize and host conferences and HR events. One such conference is a development program for middle managers. The conference has a number of professional actors from the UK to assist with knowledge transfer, role-playing, and experiential learning, in addition to the course facilitators.

All organizations have different maturity levels, priorities, budgets, capabilities, and cultures. For organizations that either do not have an L&D strategy or are looking to enhance what they currently have, I offer some tried-and-tested best-case practices from various organizations I have been a part of.

I invite you to visit my website, www.beyond-employeeengagement.com, where I have included a detailed educational table with best-case practices so organizations can begin to develop or improve their learning and development strategy and employee journey (when it comes to learning and growth) and, through that, drive performance. The table lists various learning plans that can be integrated into a holistic strategy tailored to an organization's culture. The order reflects the likely timing of implementation throughout an employee's tenure, with the first few being more applicable in the first year and the remainder being introduced later.

Indeed, for organizations just starting on their L&D journey, effectively planning and adopting all the programs outlined in the document may take a couple of years; implementing everything at once may be challenging.

PERFORMANCE MANAGEMENT—IS IT TIME TO CLOSE THAT CHAPTER?

For the last part of this chapter, let's look at how organizations can use performance appraisals for accountability and for individual and team learning and growth. We will also look at what alternatives companies are using to drive business excellence.

I am somewhat embarrassed to share this. One time, I spent an entire workday filling in my performance appraisal, specifically the section with 'remarks, examples, and justification of the score.' You may wonder why I would spend such a long time. Perhaps I didn't know how to use the clunky system. Maybe I was getting distracted. Possibly, but no. It took me so long because my manager was an exceptionally pedantic, micromanaging, nitpicking leader who would correct everyone's grammar or spelling, even in a performance appraisal. Now imagine the level of scrutiny over the self-evaluation rating! I wanted to make it bulletproof. I usually would not have been so stressed out about it, but my entire 'more-than-decent' bonus was tied up with this document, and if I achieved below a particular score, I would get zero bonus! Heavily motivated by money (don't judge me!), I diligently set out to fill in every detail, upload every document supporting my work (to the point where the system no longer allowed me to upload), and carefully craft my self-evaluation report. My colleague joked that I was writing my life story! But it was no joke. The time spent doing this appraisal, my frustration throughout the subsequent meetings (yes, multiple meetings, not just one), and de-motivation afterward must have cost the company weeks of my productivity.

You may think that not all managers are the same. And yes, that's true. But the sad truth is that many managers or leaders are not adequately equipped and trained to give proper feedback, and employees may also not be qualified enough to act on this feedback without being defensive, closed-off, or disengaged. And let's not even get started on the hours spent attending training (and mandatory refreshers) on conducting effective appraisals according to a particular organization's culture.

Other people have had completely opposite experiences. The manager would have just filled in a score and sent it to HR— no discussion, no feedback! Naturally, this does not help with the professional development of that individual.

Many of you may not know the origin of the highly unpopular performance appraisals. I was not aware that they originated from the US Military during WW1. Let's look at the timeline below in Figure 15, which was taken from "The Performance Management Revolution—The Focus Is Shifting from Accountability to Learning," an article published in the *Harvard Business Review* in October 2016 by Cappelli and Tavis.

A Talent Management Timeline

The tug-of-war between accountability and development over the decades.

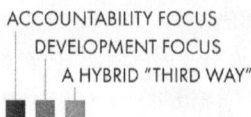

ACCOUNTABILITY FOCUS
  DEVELOPMENT FOCUS
    A HYBRID "THIRD WAY"

■ □ □	**WWI**	The U.S. military created a merit-based rating system to flag and dismiss poor performers.
□ ■ □	**WWII**	The Army devised forced ranking to identify enlisted soldiers with the potential to become officers.
■ □ □	**1940s**	About 60% of U.S. companies were using appraisals to document workers' performance and allocate rewards.
□ ■ □	**1950s**	Social psychologist Douglas McGregor argued for engaging employees in assessments and goal setting.
□ □ ■	**1960s**	Led by General Electric, companies began splitting appraisals into separate discussions about accountability and growth to give development its due.
■ □ □	**1970s**	Inflation rates shot up, and organizations felt pressure to award merit pay more objectively, so accountability again became the priority in the appraisal process.
■ □ □	**1980s**	Jack Welch championed forced ranking at GE to reward top performers, accommodate those in the middle, and get rid of those at the bottom.

■ ☐ ☐ **1990s**   McKinsey's War for Talent study pointed to a shortage of capable executives and reinforced the emphasis on assessing and rewarding performance.

■ ☐ ☐ **2000**   Organizations got flatter, which dramatically increased the number of direct reports each manager had, making it harder to invest time in developing them.

☐ ■ ☐ **2011**   Kelly Services was the first big professional services firm to drop appraisals, and other major firms followed suit, emphasizing frequent, informal feedback.

☐ ■ ☐ **2012**   Adobe ended annual performance reviews, in keeping with the famous "Agile Manifesto" and the notion that annual targets were irrelevant to the way its business operated.

☐ ☐ ■ **2016**   Deloitte, PwC, and others that tried going numberless are reinstating performance ratings but using more than one number and keeping the new emphasis on development feedback.

FIGURE 15. THE PERFORMANCE MANAGEMENT REVOLUTION

In the USA, approximately one-third of companies have replaced annual performance reviews with more frequent check-ins between managers and employees. This approach has proven more effective in promoting desired behaviors and managing performance. By providing instant feedback in a professional debriefing session and linking it to individual goals, supervisors can better monitor and improve employee performance.

Many leaders (and employees) do not see the efficacy of an annual exercise. This may be predominantly because of the long hours spent filling in the employees' appraisals, the time spent by employees filling in their self-evaluations, and then the dreaded discussion that takes place after, which oftentimes runs off topic or is conducted very inadequately.

I believe, for the most part, that performance appraisals serve no real purpose. They restrict creativity and collaboration, and the behavior may have been repeated on multiple occasions by the time the discussion has been had. They are considered by many employees as discriminatory based on gender, race, tenure, and other demographics. At times, passive-aggressive managers cannot give honest feedback, and for the sake of 'maintaining the peace' they provide an average score when that individual may have deserved a lower-than-average score. Applying the concept of bell curves and forced ranking completely demotivates high performers, as they cannot understand or disagree with the reasoning behind it.

Many businesses use a rewards and punishments system to hold their employees accountable for their past actions. However, this approach is based on a yearly cycle, which can hinder the focus on improving performance and developing talent for the future. It is vital for the organization's long-term success to shift the focus toward building a workforce that can compete both now and in the future. Regular, meaningful conversations about performance and insights into development can aid in achieving this goal. These conversations should be documented and graded (if applicable).

Perhaps we can begin (or continue) the shift by adopting a hybrid approach, where feedback is given upon completion of every significant project or milestone, or even more frequently than that. By the end of the year, the individual would have (hopefully) gathered enough constructive feedback to be able to make significant changes in their performance and sharpen their skills. If they are not performing well, then input and a plan should be given imminently, not at the end of the year. Leaders at General Electric base their discussions on two basic questions: What am I doing that I should keep doing? And: What am I doing that I should change? Frequent check-ins aim to provide immediate, detailed, constructive, and meaningful feedback from supervisors, rather than once per year during the appraisal cycle, thus creating a rich soil for individual and team improvement. Supervisors can still have an annual year-end summary discussion with their employees, and this could be a summary of all the other touchpoints that took place during the year. There would have to be formal accountability (whether at individual or team-level KPIs) and personal development measurement (behavioral and technical competency) with pre-defined tools to develop each identified competency. Formal accountability would be necessary for merit increases, bonuses, promotions, or job reassignments.

Let's tie this back to growth and development. Famous entrepreneur Garry Tan says, "At every job, you should either learn or earn. Either is fine. Both are best. But if it's neither, quit." Earlier, I proposed that one of the biggest drivers of engagement and retention is the opportunity for learning and advancement. It is a significant and ongoing part of the employee experience. If the workplace is not adding to one's basket of knowledge, their experience and that of their customers is bound to suffer. Organizations have different cultures and organizational values. One thing they all have in common is human capital (unless they are fully AI-operated). And, as humans, we like to see progress; we are fulfilled by growth and learning. For the employee experience to be rewarding for the individual, the company, and the community, it is crucial for companies to invest in their employees' ongoing learning and to create an environment of growth and prosperity for all.

So far in this book, we have discussed the touchpoints along the employee journey, including employer branding and the initial attraction, as well as the recruiting and hiring process. We have delved into onboarding, culture, employee engagement, wellbeing, internal communication, positive psychology, rewards, recognition, and motivation. Together with learning and performance, these are the major touchpoints that constitute the employee experience. But we have yet to cover the last part of the journey: the exit. We will delve into this next, followed by an entire chapter on metrics and how to measure the efficacy of all these wonderful strategies you have been putting together for the employee experience against the customer experience.

CHALLENGE ACCEPTED: PUTTING *LEARNING, DEVELOPMENT, AND PERFORMANCE* INTO ACTION

I hope you have enjoyed this chapter! How about trying these suggested tasks?

1. Personal Development Passport

Task: Work together with employees to create a personalized development passport outlining their career goals, desired skills, and learning resources. This could include online courses, conferences, mentorship opportunities, or internal training programs.

Challenge: Encourage goal setting and self-directed learning. Employees can track their progress through the passport.

Activity: Organize coaching sessions to support employees in their journey. Share success stories within the Personal Development Passport program. This empowers employees to take ownership of their learning and development journey.

2. Career Pathing Adventure

Task: Offer personalized career pathing workshop sessions, helping employees identify their strengths, aspirations, and potential career paths within the company. Provide resources and strategies for skill development and career advancement.

Challenge: Guide employees in actively shaping their professional journeys. Equip them with the tools and information to navigate internal opportunities, build relevant skills, and pursue their desired career goals.

Activity: Develop visual career path maps or online tools to empower employees to track their progress and make informed decisions about their professional development. Encourage check-ins with L&D professionals for ongoing guidance. Or organize lunch-and-learn sessions where employees can share their knowledge and expertise, fostering peer-to-peer learning and development.

3. Performance Feedback Flip

Task: Challenge traditional performance appraisal methods. Conduct workshops to explore alternative feedback approaches that focus on ongoing development, strengths appreciation, and peer-to-peer coaching.

Challenge: Move beyond one-size-fits-all annual reviews. Encourage experimentation with methods like regular check-ins, quarterly 360-degree feedback, or project-based assessments, as discussed in the chapter.

Activity: Pilot test new feedback approaches within small teams or departments. Gather feedback and iterate based on learnings. Share best practices across the organization to promote a culture of ongoing and growth-oriented performance feedback.

PART 5   Shukran, Ciao and Au Revoir

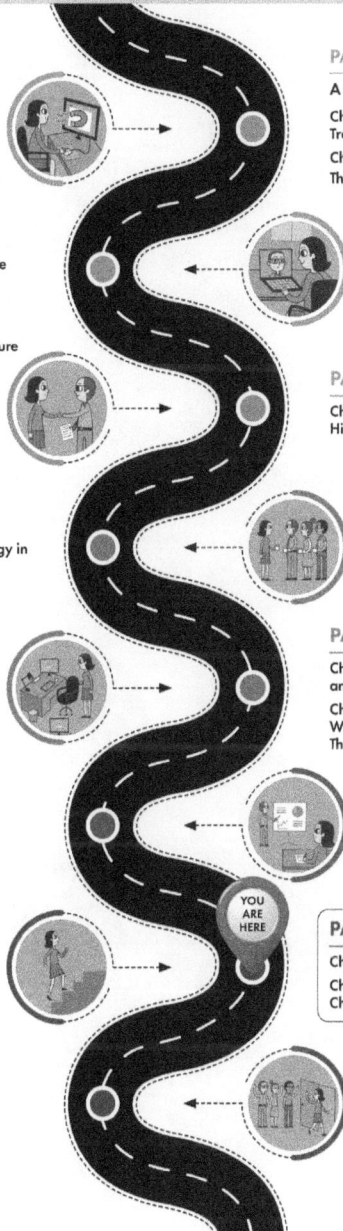

YOU ARE HERE

CHAPTER 13

THE EXIT

"Don't be long where you don't belong."

—AUTHOR UNKNOWN

I was made redundant on the 1st of May. Ironically, this date is known as Labor Day in many countries.

I often wonder, if this had not happened, would I still be in the same company? The hard truth is that I did not want to be there from day one. And the primary reason was because of the unprofessional way that my interviewing, recruiting, and onboarding processes went! I am certain that this is a situation that many of you have been in. Have you been brave enough to do something about it? Did you trap yourself into believing that having one source of income is the best way forward?

Take a moment to consider how prepared you are for job loss or business failure as an entrepreneur.

As leaders, we may have experienced employees leaving the company. On the other hand, as employees, most of us have thought about leaving a job and may even have done it. And then there are those who are entirely disgruntled about their workplace but are too scared to do something about it. They have *quietly quit* and are *comfortably miserable* in their status quo. And in the process, they may be infecting others with their disengagement.

This chapter will address the last touchpoint in the employee journey and lifecycle: exit. Sometimes, there can be re-boarding or re-joining of the company. If that is the case, then this is something that organizations should be proud of, as it is one of the highest forms of praise when an eligible employee would like to rejoin a company. It usually indicates that the company is doing something right!

We will look at the progressive disciplinary process and turn-over measurements. We will also discuss the importance of treating people with dignity, respect, and kindness throughout this last part of their journey. Always keep in mind that offboarding is as important as onboarding because as individuals leave, they continue to be brand advocates. They can either support your employer branding strategy (if you have one), or become the worst advocates of the company, which can ruin its reputation with future hires and potential clients and investors.

As a person exits the company, it is essential to encourage them to provide an honest review on Glassdoor and other platforms where future hires will be sure to research your workplace. Encouraging employees to leave a Glassdoor comment is as important as encouraging a guest to leave a Google review, a Tripadvisor review, or a comment on the company's socials. This may undoubtedly be risky and potentially backfire, especially if the employee did not have a great experience. However, maintaining honesty and transparency while officially responding to the reviews is vital. How that concern is handled also indicates the level of professionalism and care the company puts into the employee and/or customer experience. It may also be a chance to clear up any misunderstandings and misconceptions and act as an opportunity for good PR.

Let's look at three major types of departures from a company:

Termination usually refers to ending an individual's employment because they are not the right culture fit, have not passed probation, or have broken the law or the company code of ethics and conduct. Most commonly, termination results from repeated behaviors that are considered inappropriate, and in this case, the split with the company should not entirely come as a surprise. Sometimes, the offense is so severe that it requires immediate end of employment.

Employee relations departments and the manager of the person being terminated should follow the path of the progressive discipline process. This process includes coaching session(s), a verbal warning, a written warning, and a final warning following the contract's official end. The reason for this is to educate the employee and to give them the opportunity to explain their behavior and to understand the negative repercussions on the business. When followed correctly, the disciplinary process often allows for rectifying the undesired behavior. If the behavior hasn't changed after repeated alerts and coaching, termination may need to follow.

The termination process should be taken seriously and conducted with utmost ethics and confidentiality. Keep in mind that, at times, the individual may be a wrong departmental fit or a wrong hire, which could be an error on the part of the talent acquisition team. This is why it is important for both parties to understand the reason behind a particular behavior.

Many leaders say, 'hire slow and fire fast,' but I urge you to consider the repercussions of your actions before you exert your power to change someone's life. In some of the companies I've worked at, we used a performance management grid to categorize offenses and their repercussions. This helped to ensure fairness, equity, consistency with the decisions, and transparency in the process.

Redundancy: This also includes furlough, restructuring, and downsizing.

Terminations, redundancies, and resignations change individuals' lives and the lives of their families and communities. However, they also affect the company culture. Separation from a company (whether voluntary or involuntary) costs money in terms of a severance package, overtime for people replacing that individual, and new hiring costs. It also has emotional, psychological, and organizational repercussions. Consider the cost of brain drain, a change in culture, and a blow to the psychological safety of those employees left behind.

Have you heard of workplace survivor syndrome? Organizational psychologists coined this term to explain the feelings of employees who remain in the middle of company downsizing. Some common feelings are anger, guilt, and mistrust.

HR professionals, managers, and leaders should never undertake a termination/redundancy lightly or without proper planning. After all, this is a major touchpoint that shapes the overall employee experience, and it should be done professionally. Throughout my career, I have learned some crucial steps that must be followed to deliver a professional employee experience, even during hard times. Unfortunately, I have had to carry out hundreds of terminations and redundancies and have received hundreds of resignations. As a consultant, I have also led company closures that resulted in mass redundancies. It is never an easy process and must be done with precision, compassion, and professionalism.

When planning for such eventualities, I advise establishing a solid plan to help navigate workforce reduction and result in as little trauma as possible. The plan should also aim to psychologically prepare the team who is performing the operation: they deliver the news and must be fully prepared to deliver it with dignity, respect, and kindness. The second part of the plan involves the aftermath and the PR, as well as the employee branding and the employer branding. Planning reduces risk and stress during a very difficult time.

Here are the four phases of a layoff:

Phase 1—Making the Decision: This process must consider all eventualities of the decision, including the influence on the remaining workforce, the legalities, the effect on diversity and inclusion, and the future financial stability of an organization. Heads of departments should be consulted when finalizing the list, and this must be kept strictly confidential. Don't allow the rumor mill to get ahead of you and influence the process.

Phase 2—Planning and Preparation: This phase must include all the applicable internal and external pre- and post-communication plans for crisis communication and the modes of interaction with all employees throughout the process. All the necessary paperwork must be ready and printed for signing during the meeting, including the severance package. Please remember to include the manager of the individual being laid off in the meeting; this is both professional and reassuring. If the manager has never been present during such a meeting, they must be given complete transparency on the project and training on handling the meeting and the weeks after it. The meetings must be appropriately scheduled, and the location must be neutral and private. A script and talking points should be followed for consistency.

Phase 3—Managing Notification Day: Depending on the organization's size, this may take several days or weeks. Is there a plan for remote workers and those on leave? Does your company have an employee assistance program (EAP)? In one of my workplaces, we organized on-site counselors and psychologists. During one of the meetings, the colleague who was being terminated fainted, and we had to call an ambulance! Sometimes, the news sinks in a few days after the meeting, and anxiety and despair may follow. Something else that's very important is carefully granting access to the office, the workstations, emails/company-issued technology, and the process of allowing affected colleagues to say goodbye to their teammates. Make sure you think all eventualities through in a humane and compassionate way.

Phase 4—Leading Company Recovery: This can include town halls and departmental meetings with senior leadership present if necessary, during which time the remaining team is provided with clear direction about the future and the business reasons behind the decisions. At this point, empathy and professionalism from the HR team and the managers of the affected departments are essential. They must be well-trained and empowered to take an active interest in employee concerns. In one of my previous workplaces, we provided proactive training on writing CVs, interviewing skills, and job-search strategies. We also provided a list of companies specializing in recruitment and headhunting. Have you considered how to support the mental health of affected managers and HR teams delivering the news if you're not using an external company?

Resignation: Unlike terminations and redundancies, a resignation is usually voluntary. It includes voluntary departures, such as retirement and cross-boarding from one entity to another.

Certain company cultures encourage the celebration of someone's departure through a farewell gathering, especially if the individual leaving has been with the company for a long time. This is a beautiful practice, and I strongly encourage creating a culture of celebration and appreciation at your workplace; don't be afraid to acknowledge the smallest of things, even though they may not seem significant. On the contrary, they are meaningful to at least one person. In the case of a departure, this is a momentous time for the person and the team they are leaving.

You might even be brave enough to take things a step further and organize a farewell for those colleagues who have been made redundant! This is a very sensitive topic and must only be considered if your company culture supports it, as you do not want to seem insensitive or attract cynicism.

Often, resignations can allow us to gather insights into the department's wellbeing and the manager's effectiveness. This brings me to the next essential part of this chapter: data gathering and reporting—and even more importantly, what we do with this data.

THIS COULD BE YOUR LAST CHANCE

There can be multiple reasons why a person chooses to leave a company. Data from various reputed sources such as McKinsey & Company and MIT Sloan Management Review indicate that people leave their jobs because of disrespectful cultures, non-inclusive climates, and leaders who do not care for their teams. Understanding these reasons helps authentically improve the middle part of the employee experience (the engage, grow, and perform touchpoints), specifically for those individuals still working in the company. This helps ensure that the customer experience is positively affected by an outstanding employee experience.

A professional HR team aims to gather feedback from the onset of the employee journey: the attracting, interviewing, selecting, hiring, and onboarding phases. They also gather feedback through various other surveys aimed at measuring engagement, trust, satisfaction, and opinions. The last chance to gather feedback from an employee is during the departure stage of the journey.

There are various ways to do that, including an exit survey and an in-depth exit interview following the survey. What we do with this qualitative and quantitative data is essential to workplace betterment. The last chapter discusses this in more detail, concentrating entirely on measurement. If the HR team, as well as the organization's leaders, use this data in an intelligent way, they can prevent further voluntary turnover, help preserve the culture, and guarantee high levels of engagement, motivation, and productivity; they can also ensure that future hires have an even better employee experience, which could very possibly result in a great customer experience!

IT MIGHT NOT BE YOUR LAST CHANCE

Organizations that prioritize their employee experience recognize the value of their company alumni: those who have departed but may one day return. By dedicating time, energy, and resources to promoting their culture, companies ensure that valuable employees who leave voluntarily for personal reasons are not lost forever. Loyalty and commitment are rare, and it's essential to develop programs that keep alumni feeling appreciated, engaged, and nurtured. Educational institutions and student organizations like AIESEC have long implemented this practice globally, and it's time for companies to follow suit. By utilizing platforms designed to maintain emotional connections with previous employees, companies can (re)attract their leavers, as well as positively impact their employer branding and inspire loyalty and commitment in all who work there.

IN THE END

It is a fact that people leave their bosses. They also leave organizations. Workplaces that take the time to understand the *real* reasons behind a voluntary departure and continuously act thoughtfully and authentically on the feedback given to them will be able to build environments that promote an outstanding employee experience. This will result in an extraordinary customer experience.

Of course, some might say that it's too late to gather feedback from people who are leaving and that they should have offered their input before deciding to resign. Maybe they did. Maybe no one listened. Before heading to the next chapter, which will focus on the metrics one can adopt to measure the strategies implemented in previous sections, let's do a quick recap of the key learnings on the last stage of the employee journey: the exit.

The three types of departure from a company are generally categorized under redundancies, resignations, and terminations. For any type of departure, whether voluntary or involuntary, it is essential for the HR team in charge, as well as the head of the department, to be fully involved in the process and to be prepared for all eventualities. For terminations, it is recommended that you follow the progressive disciplinary process so that employees can have a chance to learn from their mistakes unless they are breaking the law or going against the code of business conduct. Following an approved document aligned with all internal policies is essential to ensure equity and transparency in the disciplinary process.

Lastly, remember that an employee who has left your organization has valuable feedback that you will want to hear and act upon if you want to prevent further resignations or, even worse, having a disgruntled person on the team who is affecting the rest. Always listen to feedback with an open mind and ensure that your brand advocates, even those departing the company, leave feeling respected and knowing that their voice still matters. In one of the organizations that I have begun to consult, we have implemented an interesting twist on exit interviews and surveys. We conduct the standard research prior to their departure, but then we also contact the departed candidate after six months for another discussion, if they are agreeable. It is very interesting to note that at least half of the resigned employees change their story and their reasons for leaving, once they speak to HR six months later. There is so much new learning from the new discussion! It also goes to show that there is little psychological safety in that company and that there is a lot of work to be done.

Throughout this book, I have identified all the touchpoints that affect the employee experience. By doing that, I hope that you now understand how to create an outstanding employee experience so that you can guarantee an exceptional customer experience. The next chapter aims to inspire you to use scientific evidence as the basis of your employee experience strategy.

CHALLENGE ACCEPTED: PUTTING *THE EXIT* INTO ACTION

Here are some suggested activities you can engage in once you have absorbed the learning from this chapter.

1. Exit Interview Empathy Lab

Task: Train HR professionals on conducting effective exit interviews that go beyond collecting facts and delve into deeper emotions and motivations behind employee departures. Train on conducting in-depth conversations to improve the employee journey.

Challenge: Develop active listening skills, understand unspoken cues, and encourage genuine open dialogue during exit interviews. Use insights to identify recurring patterns and address underlying concerns impacting employee retention.

Activity: Organize role-playing exercises and simulations to practice conducting impactful exit interviews.

2. Reverse Onboarding Retreat

Task: Conduct a reverse onboarding retreat where new employees share their initial experiences, challenges, and suggestions for improving the onboarding process.

Challenge: Gain fresh perspectives from new hires and identify areas for improvement.

Activity: Facilitate interactive sessions where new employees can voice their feedback and suggestions. Celebrate implemented changes and showcase the impact of reverse onboarding on future new hire experiences.

3. Talent Alumni Network Launch

Task: Establish a dedicated alumni network for former employees to stay connected with the company, share expertise, and potentially return in the future.

Challenge: Build a lasting connection with talented individuals who have left the company. Develop an engaging alumni platform, organize virtual or in-person gatherings, and provide mentorship opportunities for ongoing knowledge exchange and collaboration between current and former employees.

Activity: Showcase success stories of rehired employees that benefit the individuals and the organization. This fosters a culture of appreciation for past experience and encourages ongoing connection with former employees.

CHAPTER 14

THE METRICS CHAPTER

"What gets measured, gets managed."

—PETER DRUCKER

How many articles have you read on 'The Great Resignation,' 'The Great Attrition', 'Quiet Quitting,' 'Contagious Quitting,' or perhaps 'The Cost of Turnover'?

Yes, these terms are all true; they are not myths. They are detrimental to an organization, its people, and its societies. We can even look at how employee disengagement affects a country's culture. Yes, you read right! Look at the big picture here: Imagine an instance where companies don't pay their employees well; provide workplace flexibility, growth, or development; instill a sense of genuine care, belonging, recognition, and appreciation; or offer competitive benefits. This is one reason countries experience brain drain, which describes the emigration of skilled labor to other countries for better pay and living conditions. Many countries are experiencing a loss of highly educated people and unskilled labor. This happens worldwide. And that's why so many expatriates live in countries like the United Arab Emirates. This country listens to and cares for its population, encouraging companies to consider workers' wellbeing and enabling them to form a diverse and inclusive workplace. Having been in the UAE for over 16 years, I can undoubtedly say that the leaders of this country evidently care. However, it's not just the leaders—it's the organizations, too.

Why do they care? And more importantly, why *should* they care? To deliver a better customer experience (and make money), of course! Happy and engaged employees provide outstanding customer service, resulting in repeat clientele and increased revenue. However, this is not the only reason. As more companies turn to sustainability and adding value to communities and people's lives, they begin to appreciate that employees must be treated well in all aspects. It became more evident throughout the pandemic and post-pandemic period that individuals are not only in need of a paycheck. They look at work for connection, meaning, belonging, and mattering. They look at work for interactions, not just transactions.

Now, how do we know that? Because of the millions of surveys administered by research giants such as Gallup, McKinsey & Company, Qualtrics, and Culture Amp. And why should we continue to measure all of this? Because as management guru Peter Drucker rightfully said, "What gets measured, gets managed."

Throughout this book, we have looked at the how and the why concerning each touchpoint along the employee experience journey. Now it's time to understand how to assess the efficacy of your work on the employee experience so that you can manage it even better in the long term and continue to build legendary workplace cultures. This chapter will help readers further understand the necessity of creating and maintaining an excellent employee experience and how that relates to a remarkable customer experience. It will showcase several scientific ways in which this can be proven. Often, the buy-in isn't there—or if it is, then it may not be fully there.

Listening to the employee's voice once a year is simply not enough! Employee feedback must be obtained regularly and continuously throughout the employee lifecycle. The listening strategy must create an active dialogue and capture real-time employee experience feedback. But most importantly, organizations must act on the feedback they have received.

In this penultimate chapter, we look at the qualitative and quantitative research companies can engage in to listen, understand, evaluate, and learn from their employees' voices. Acting on this feedback is key.

Why do people leave an organization? What are the intentions compelling individuals to stay in an organization? And what is significant to them? Including the voice of employees indicates a company's intent to involve them in planning, aligning, and shaping the organization, thus demonstrating that their opinions and well-being matter.

We touch on other analytics, such as those which can be obtained through social media, websites, and company intranets. We also look at productivity, absenteeism, and attrition metrics. We end with qualitative research—namely focus groups and interviews.

Gathering metrics, analyzing them, and making improvements based on the findings will provide the necessary tools to increase budgets and headcounts, gain buy-in where needed, and present a scientifically backed study on why having a department dedicated to managing all aspects of the employee experience is vital. Moreover, leaders cannot fix what they don't know or what they don't understand. This is why we need metrics showing a positive correlation between the employee experience and the customer experience.

HOW TO ASSESS YOUR TEAMS AND YOUR WORK IN A QUANTITATIVE WAY

Quantitative feedback comes from surveys, and qualitative feedback is derived from in-depth focus groups, one-on-one interviews, and year-on-year studies of human behavior.

Surveys can indicate where your workforce currently is from a collective perspective (meaning how engaged or happy employees are with your organization), but they can also tell you how engaged they are with life in general from an individual perspective. Ideally, you would conduct a healthy mix of both types of surveys.

Surveying all the touchpoints throughout the employee journey is paramount to assessing where you stand and forming a strategy for continuous improvement.

I have compiled a thorough template that can be found on my website, www.beyond-employeeengagement.com. It shows you how to continuously measure progress. There, you will find a variety of surveys that can assess your current organizational state. Administered effectively and consistently, their results may indicate improvement or deterioration over time. I would advise putting together an organic quantitative and qualitative listening strategy that works well with your corporate culture and respects your organization's current readiness. This strategy should ideally be communicated at the beginning of each year, together with the annual goals and key performance indicators (KPIs).

From a quantitative perspective, the best way to do this is to put together a detailed calendar that shows the big picture of all the surveys you aim to administer throughout the year. This sets the tone and demonstrates to the employees that you are serious about listening and acting on their feedback. I hope you find this blueprint useful!

To evaluate the employee experience, it is imperative to track, measure, and evaluate how people are *actually* doing, not just how they *say* they are doing. Engagement surveys are an excellent way of measuring progress, but sometimes employees may only say what they *think* they should be feeling. This is why data from engagement surveys may not indicate the full, authentic picture. Consider this: engagement is cyclical, and colleagues may feel differently today than they felt last week or last month. How accurate do you think your data will be if you conduct surveys annually and don't include pulse surveys throughout the year? Actions speak louder than words. What people say is just as important as what they do not say. For this reason, I cannot stress enough the importance of genuinely getting to know your employees and understanding what matters to them.

Another, more in-depth way of doing this is through qualitative focus groups and one-on-one interviews.

THE QUALITATIVE WAY

Throughout my career, I have conducted hundreds of focus groups. I love them because they allow me to ask follow-up questions to people's survey responses and dig deep to understand specific issues. Even better are personal interviews because you can focus on one individual. The advantage of surveys is that they allow you to gather feedback from a large audience relatively quicker than focus groups or one-on-one discussions do. However, qualitative research gives deeper insight.

I recommend building a hybrid listening strategy that supports both research methods. A well-established listening strategy promotes healthy three-way communication in an organization. These surveys (and questions) are one way an organization can communicate with its employees. The types of questions asked indicate what is important to an organization. Employees' responses complete the two-way communication loop. This is called top-to-bottom and bottom-to-top communication. If you take this further, conversations prompted by surveys allow lateral communication between employees.

Focus groups foster even more effective three-way communication. As discussed in the chapter on internal communication, timely, frequent, honest three-way communication builds engagement and trust and is a vital component of the employee experience.

Focus groups and individual interviews can be conducted on a variety of topics. Visit my website,

www.beyond-employeeengagement.com, to look at the detailed template on qualitative research. It includes information for conducting focus groups and various types of personal interviews with employees along their work journey and incorporates suggestions for focus groups with new joiners who have completed probation, wellbeing and cultural assessments, management and leadership evaluations, stay and exit interviews, and assessments of strategies pertaining to internal comms, Rewards and Recognition, and so much more.

DASHBOARDS, DIGITAL METRICS, AND OTHERS

Usually, analytics educate us on the status of our processes so we can measure a baseline and define successes, improvements, and failures along every touchpoint of the employee journey. Now that we have looked at qualitative and quantitative research, let's move on to digital metrics and other systems measuring the employee experience. These may be useful alerts for HR professionals, managers, and leaders to further support evaluating the employee experience and how it correlates to the customer experience. This could be, for instance, repeated issues with customer satisfaction in a particular department, which could be directly attributed to increased absenteeism, sick leave, and a decreased employee engagement score—or the opposite: an impressive total motivation (ToMo) score and a remarkable net promoter score (NPS) in the same department.

These metrics can be represented on business dashboards and include data such as:

- sick leave days
- absenteeism
- employee relations incidents
- official grievances about a particular leader
- customer satisfaction: e.g. NPS, mystery shopper score
- customer complaints on external platforms such as Tripadvisor
- overall customer loyalty and repeat clientele vs. other outlets/entities/subsidiaries
- employee productivity scores, complete/incomplete KPIs/annual goals

- financials: revenue, profit, sales, and upselling targets
- employee turnover and the cost of attrition
- internal vs. external hires, readiness for promotions, quality of pipeline for internal talent
- how internal communication influences employees
- digital comms analytics (such as where, how, and with what they access a platform, what content they read, what pages they visit, topics they prefer, videos watched, and average time watched), clicks on company newsletters, what communication channels are used the most, etc. (the chapter on internal communication talks about this in detail)
- participation in company events or volunteering.

What story do the actions of your employees portray? What indicators do you use to measure their experience and their engagement and connection to the company?

Assessing a company's internal reputation or employee brand is crucial. However, it's equally important to measure the external reputation or employer brand of a company, as it reflects how well an organization can attract, retain, engage, and develop talent. To evaluate this aspect, companies can use key metrics such as social media, the intranet, awards such as Top Employer and WELL certification, and audits. Winning industry awards is also an excellent measure of a company's external reputation.

Companies can also turn to other measurements directly linked to their employer brand. I borrowed this concise diagram from the Academy to Innovate HR, which perfectly illustrates the many ways to measure that.

Candidate NPS

ROI of employer branding

Employee referral rate

Candidate demographics

Cost per hire

12 Employer Branding Metrics to Know

Offer acceptance rate

Social engagement

Glassdoor interview experience

Candidate quality

Employer brand index

Career page Analytics

Open applications/ Expressions of interest

FIGURE 16. TWELVE EMPLOYER BRANDING METRICS TO KNOW

In addition to the employer brand, it is vital to assess the reputation of your company brand and see what your customers think of you. This can be done through surveys, one-on-one in-depth interviews, industry awards, benchmarking, reputation trackers, company growth rates, and assessing a loyalty program's success.

SO NOW WHAT?

Doing all or some of what was just discussed will give you a holistic picture of your organization. Perhaps you're happy with that, but perhaps you are not assessing the voice of your employees at all. When you do evaluate it, it might be shockingly bad.

Maybe, just like Ebenezer Scrooge in Charles Dickens' 1843 novella *A Christmas Carol*, you may feel ashamed of your actions and wish to make a change. Perhaps, by looking at the analytics we discussed earlier, you will be able to see how you can transform your organization to better serve your internal and external customers. It's only a possibility, but it's worth considering how the ghosts of Christmas Past, Christmas Present, and Christmases Yet to Come might help you become a better organization.

However, don't feel overwhelmed or obliged to introduce loads of qualitative and quantitative research to your agenda. If you do, your employees may feel like lab mice! The templates on my website are good case-practice examples of how a company can gather and assess feedback and continuously work on improvement. It is critical to connect all this data to a story and integrate it with all the touchpoints of the employee journey. The research should be balanced and factor in the organization's current maturity level, culture, and readiness. The different types of data collection should be introduced in a progressive manner. Sometimes, you don't need a survey to know something needs changing. Once you make those changes, you can then use surveys to see what people think. If possible, though, it's better to begin with a survey or a focus group to establish a baseline. Measure, analyze, identify, inform, act, and remind—this is what it means to develop a culture of feedback.

If people in your organization do not respond to surveys, you must find out why. It may be a result of survey fatigue, or it may be a result of survey mistrust. Sometimes, workplaces have a reputation for not upholding confidentiality or for not acting on the feedback after conducting the research. Colleagues may not believe that their opinion matters.

This is why what you do with the results is more important than the results themselves. Be sure to tell your people what you will be doing and remind them what has been done. This is a perfect time to use the three-percent rule strategy shared in the internal communication chapter. As a reminder, this rule suggests that 3% of people in an organization shape the perceptions of the other 90%! Companies are encouraged to identify the informal influencers inside their organizations and use them to help shape the emotions of the group to accelerate mindset change.

Engaged employees and high-performing organizations are not mutually exclusive. In fact, investing in one can positively impact the other. When planning and executing a listening strategy, it's fundamental to connect trends and insights to business outcomes, such as revenue, repeat clientele, client retention rate, customer satisfaction, and employee turnover, to mention a few.

An active listening strategy should include a plan for targeted interventions, which will demonstrate to employees that their feedback is used to drive change. This enables employee engagement, motivation, and productivity.

This chapter has discussed the internal and external methods used to measure various metrics. We have looked at the difference between qualitative and quantitative research and how it can be applied to measure the overall employee experience and to hear and act upon the voice of the employees. Combined, these measurements will tell a story.

I invite you to think about this now: What story is your organization telling? How can your actions influence this story?

CHALLENGE ACCEPTED: PUTTING *MEASUREMENT* INTO ACTION

Here are some strategic activities that you will find are instrumental in measuring and managing your entire employee experience strategy. They will help build a detailed roadmap for a data-driven and collaborative approach to the employee journey. This will empower teams to create a work environment where individual contributions are valued and connected to the bigger picture, fostering motivation, engagement, and a shared sense of purpose within the organization.

1. Metrics Makeover Mission

Task: Conduct a thorough review of existing HR metrics. Challenge the relevance and accuracy of current metrics and explore alternative indicators that better align with organizational goals and employee wellbeing.

Challenge: Focus on holistic measures that capture various aspects of employee performance, engagement, and development. Prioritize actionable metrics.

Activity: Organize focus groups to gather employee feedback on existing metrics and suggest potential improvements. Collaborate with data analysts and HR professionals from other organizations to refine metrics, develop dashboards, and track progress.

2. Storytelling with Stats

Task: Train the HR team on how to communicate complex data effectively.

Challenge: Aim to translate numbers into impactful stories that capture attention, highlight key trends, and inspire engagement with data-driven initiatives.

Activity: Organize workshops on data storytelling techniques. Encourage the team to practice translating data into narratives using real-world examples and case studies.

3. Metrics Mosaic Challenge

Task: Encourage cross-functional collaboration between HR and other departments to identify KPIs that align with broader organizational goals and strategic priorities.

Challenge: Break down departmental silos and foster a culture of data-driven collaboration. Ensure metrics are aligned across different functions and contribute to a unified understanding of employee impact.

Activity: Organize workshops where representatives from different departments discuss organizational goals and collaboratively identify relevant KPIs. Develop a shared metrics mosaic that connects individual employee performance to broader organizational objectives. Use this as a living document that should adapt to changing business priorities, technological advancements, and employee needs. Regularly review and refine the metrics to ensure they remain relevant.

CHAPTER 15

CONCLUSIONS: WHEN PEOPLE FEEL BETTER, THEY DO BETTER

Earlier in this book, I shared a story about my 40th birthday party. That experience was truly remarkable and unforgettable. Throughout these pages, I have elaborated on the key concepts that were present at that event, all of which are integral to designing an exceptional employee experience—everything from intentionality and purposefulness to connectedness, involvement, authenticity, reliability, consistency, sustainability, immersion, unpredictability, excitement, and psychological safety. Each of these constructs is a vital ingredient in creating a workplace that is exceptional.

Throughout my research, I drew inspiration from Pine and Gilmore's Four Realms of Experience and Tarssanen's Experience Pyramid Model to develop my own blueprint for creating an exceptional employee experience that drives a remarkable customer experience. In my approach, I focus on mass-customizing the journey according to the audience while keeping an eye out for opportunities to create transformational experiences. To achieve this, I recommend enhancing and innovating the services offered by the company, theming the elements, adding positive cues, eliminating negative cues, and engaging all five senses. Additionally, I recommend considering how to positively impact the motivational, physical, intellectual, emotional, and mental levels of both internal and external customers. These strategies can create an experience that resonates with our audience and leaves a lasting positive impression, resulting in overall success.

The definition of a successful company has transcended mere financial gains; it hinges on the positive influence a company wields over society. In this transformative era, crafting and fostering an exceptional employee experience takes center stage, for it holds the key to corporate prosperity and our global community's advancement.

In our quest to create an extraordinary employee experience, we uncover a treasure trove of possibilities. First and foremost among them is the creation of a workplace where every individual feels psychologically safe and respected, a place where every employee is not just a cog in the machine but a valued contributor. This entails implementing policies that champion diversity and inclusion and avenues for personal and professional growth. Additionally, cultivating open communication and trust is paramount. In the fertile soil of trust, employees find the inspiration to rise to their highest potential. When employees feel valued and heard, their engagement and motivation soar. This is achieved by encouraging feedback and involving employees in decision-making.

Furthermore, the magic of a legendary employee experience is achievable through an intentional focus on the touchpoints that form their employee journey. I defined those touchpoints as attracting, identifying, hiring, onboarding, engaging, growing, performing, and exiting. I shared my expertise on creating unique experiences at each stage to help companies achieve better results. I also suggested incorporating elements of positive psychology to enhance positive organizational behavior and positive organizational scholarship during the engaging touchpoint. Additionally, I proposed a three-way internal communication strategy framework and emphasized the importance of building a company culture on the backbone of organizational values, wellbeing, rewards, recognition, and motivation. Prioritizing employee wellbeing not only attracts and retains top talent but also instills a sense of purpose. Lastly, I highlighted the value of alumni as employee advocates who can help enhance the employee brand and may even return to work for the organization in the future. By focusing on these touchpoints and incorporating these strategies, companies can create exceptional employee experience journeys.

But why does all this matter? The profound connection between creating an extraordinary employee experience and improving society lies in the simple truth that companies are not mere economic entities. They are integral to our communities, capable of fostering equity and belonging by prioritizing their employees' wellbeing and happiness.

Moreover, it's not just about the now; it's about the enduring legacy of success. By investing in our employees, we cultivate fertile ground, creating a rich culture of innovation and excellence. This culture motivates employees to excel beyond the ordinary and ultimately results in heightened productivity and superior products, services, and customer experiences. In the end, it translates to enduring financial prosperity.

Creating an exceptional employee experience is not just sound business practice; it's also a means to enhance society. By nurturing a culture of open communication, companies attract top talent, improve financial outcomes, and play a transformative role in the world. In today's interconnected landscape, where business triumph and societal responsibility converge, prioritizing the employee experience is the path to thriving and making a meaningful impact. It is a step on the path to a more equitable world.

This book echoes these sentiments as it explores the art of crafting legendary employee experiences that lead to phenomenal customer experiences. Its purpose extends beyond enhancing customer interactions; it's about cultivating engaged individuals and vibrant societies. According to the *State of the Global Workplace*

Report by Gallup, research on workplace wellbeing has found that having a job one dislikes is more detrimental than being unemployed. This negativity can also affect people's personal lives and relationships with their families. If someone is not doing well at work, it is unlikely they will be doing well in life as a whole.

Throughout these chapters, I have outlined essential steps for organizations to create positive employee and customer experiences. By embracing these steps, employees at all levels contribute to an environment where individuals feel valued and invested.

Increasingly, we feel the importance of belonging, both professionally and societally. This is evident in the growing demand for recognition and appreciation. It is also reflected in a 71% increase in diversity and inclusion roles on LinkedIn, as reported by Glint over the past five years. The need for inclusion is especially pronounced in the workplace, where individuals invest significant time and energy. It underscores the necessity of fostering an environment that champions diversity, equity, equality, and inclusivity, where every voice is respected and supported. This ethos not only benefits employees but also enhances the organization's overall performance, which spurs productivity, innovation, and holistic success.

This book is also about creating a psychologically safe work environment, a place where people enjoy their work because they are kept well-informed and they know their voice matters. It's about fostering a culture of genuine care, appreciation, and kindness, a culture where people can grow their careers through their strengths and positively impact their personal lives. A place where people connect meaningfully and are happy to show up. A place where one feels their organization goes above and beyond to nurture a remarkable workplace for them. A place that inspires them to bring their best selves every day and to deliver their best to their customers.

In closing, this book invites you to ponder how your company's societal contribution can be magnified through the creation of an extraordinary employee experience. An experience beyond employee engagement. It's a journey that transcends organizational boundaries, enriching lives, fortifying communities, and sparking transformative change.

I invite workplaces to embark on this journey, for it's a voyage toward prosperity, purpose, and profound societal transformation.

A note to my reader

Dear Esteemed Reader,

If you found my book to be a valuable addition to your literary collection, I kindly invite you to share your thoughts by leaving a review on Amazon. Your feedback is immensely appreciated and contributes to the ongoing dialogue between authors and readers.

Your support not only means the world to me but also helps fellow readers make informed decisions.

Thank you for being part of this literary journey.

If you liked this book ...

Ready to Ignite the Power of People? Let's Take Action Together!

You've reached the end of this book, but your journey to empower people and transform workplaces is just beginning. The words you've encountered throughout these pages are your launchpad for action. Ready to put theory into practice and create a ripple effect of positive change? Go for it!

And if you need help, I'm here to partner with you every step of the way.

- Need expert guidance? My consulting services delve deep into your unique needs, crafting bespoke strategies for employee engagement, performance optimization, and organizational development.
- Empower your team through training. Interactive workshops and engaging sessions unlock the potential within your people, equipping them with the skills and knowledge to thrive.
- Let's co-create your future. My expertise in strategy formation helps you chart a clear course for your organization, aligned with your vision and fueled by data-driven insights.
- Invite me to share my passion. As a speaker, I ignite audiences with actionable ideas and inspire them to build workplaces where people and purpose intertwine.

What can I collaborate with you on?

Boost Bottom Line & Performance

- Increased employee engagement: My strategies demonstrably reduce turnover, enhance productivity, and improve customer satisfaction, leading to direct financial gains.
- Data-driven decision making: I translate complex metrics into actionable insights, optimizing resource allocation and driving ROI-focused initiatives.
- Unleash innovation: My approach fosters a culture of creativity and problem-solving, leading to breakthrough ideas and competitive advantage.
- Reduce operational costs: My training programs enhance efficiency, streamline processes, and minimize workplace issues, freeing up resources for growth.

Strengthen Leadership & Culture

- Attract and retain top talent: My expertise helps you build a desirable employer brand, attracting and retaining high-performing individuals.
- Develop future leaders: My leadership development programs equip high-potential employees with the skills and confidence to navigate future challenges.
- Cultivate a positive work environment: I foster a culture of trust, respect, and psychological safety, boosting employee wellbeing and motivation.

Stay Ahead of the Curve

- Future-proof your workforce: I equip your team with the necessary skills and mindset to thrive in the ever-changing business landscape.
- Build data-driven agility: My employee experience framework helps you leverage data to adapt quickly to market shifts and seize emerging opportunities.
- Shape the future of work: I collaborate with you to create a human-centric workplace that attracts and inspires the next generation of talent.

But the journey doesn't end here. My website overflows with bonus resources, downloadable templates, and exclusive insights I couldn't fit within these pages.

Remember, the greatest impact unfolds when we join forces. Let's collaborate and create a world where every employee thrives, every organization boasts a legendary employee experience and a phenomenal customer experience, and ultimately, every community enjoys the power of positive change.

I'm on a mission to inspire and promote happiness. And yes, I got it from my grandma!

With gratitude,
Kristina Vaneva

Email: kristinavaneva@hotmail.com
LinkedIn: linkedin.com/in/kristinavaneva
Website: www.beyond-employeeengagement.com

REFERENCES

Chapter 3: The Customer Experience in the Experience Economy

Pine, B. J., & Gilmore, H. J. (1998). *The experience economy*. Harvard Business School Press.

Pine, B. J., & Gilmore, H. J. (2001). *The experience economy: Work is theatre and every business a stage* (Updated edition). Harvard Business School Press.

Pine, B. J., & Gilmore, H. J. (2011). *The experience economy: Authenticity: What consumers really want* (Updated edition). Harvard Business School Press.

Pine, B. J., & Gilmore, H. J. (2013). The experience economy, past present, and future. In J. Sundbo & F. Sorensen (Eds.), *Handbook on the experience economy*. Edward Elgar Publishing (Ltd).

Tarssanen, S. (2009). *Handbook for experience stagers* (5th ed). LEO, Lapland Center of Expertise for the Experience Industry.

Chapter 4: The Employee Experience Journey

Cochran, J. Virtual Interview through Zoom on September 18, 2021

Finnegan Institute. Retrieved June 13, 2021, from https://www.finneganinstitute.com/

Finnegan Institute. Retrieved July 19, 2021, from https://www.finneganinstitute.com/courses-catalog/calculating-cost-turnover/

Gallup. Retrieved September 3, 2021, from https://www.gallup.com/workplace/323573/employee-experience-and-workplace-culture.aspx

Gallup. Retrieved July 17, 2023, from https://www.gallup.com/workplace/349484/state-of-the-global-workplace.aspx

iOffice Hummingbird. *Using technology in the workplace. Elevating employee experience.* Retrieved August 24, 2021, from https://cdn2.hubspot.net/hubfs/32387/2018/PDFs/EmployeeExperience_eBOOK.pdf

Morgan, J. (2010). *The future of work.* John Willey & Sons.

Morgan, J. (2012). *The collaborative organization.* McGraw Hill.

Morgan, J. (2017). *The employee experience advantage.* John Wiley & Sons.

The Future Organization. Retrieved May 1, 2023, from https://thefutureorganization.com/

Unily. Retrieved September 25, 2023, from https://www.unily.com/

Chapter 5: A Company Culture—Inception, Living It, and Transformations

Barrett Values Centre. Retrieved October 10, 2022, from https://www.valuescentre.com

Dinovo, R. (2020). *The culture builders.* Self-published.

Friedman, D. (2018). *Culture by Design: 8 simple steps to drive better individual and organizational performance.* Infinity Publishing.

Indeed. Retrieved May 20, 2023, from https://www.indeed.com/career-advice/career-development/culture-assessment

PwC. Retrieved May 20, 2023, from https://www.pwc.com/gx/en/issues/upskilling/global-culture-survey-2021.html

Razzetti, G. *Future-Proof Your Company Culture Webinar.* Retrieved December 5, 2023, from https://www.youtube.com/watch?v=hu_G3QEOi24

World of Work Project. Retrieved May 20, 2023, from https://worldofwork.io/2019/07/organizational-culture-assessment-questionnaire/

Chapter 6: Attract, Identify, Hire, Onboard

Academy to Innovate HR. Retrieved May 13, 2023, from https://www.aihr.com/blog/employer-branding-metrics/

Fraser Dove International. Retrieved May 11, 2023, from https://www.fraserdove.com/measure-employer-brand/

Harvard Business Review. Retrieved February 6, 2023, from https://hbr.org/2018/01/why-people-really-quit-their-jobs

Link Humans. Retrieved May 14, 2023, from https://linkhumans.com/employer-brand-index/

Silkroad Technology and CareerBuilder. Retrieved May 13, 2023, from https://hr1.silkroad.com/state-of-recruitment-onboarding

Talent Lyft. Retrieved May 14, 2023, from https://www.talentlyft.com/en/resources/employer-branding-survey-questions

Chapter 7: Engage

Bakker, A. B., van Emmerik, H., & Euwema, M. C. (2006). Crossover of burnout and engagement in work teams. *Work and Occupations, 33*, 464–489.

Bellah, R. N., Madsen, R., Sullivan, W. M., Swidler, A., & Tripton, S. M. (1985). *Habits of the heart.* University of California Press.

Buckinghamshire Five Ways Resource Pack. (2008). Retrieved September 1, 2022, from http://www.bucks.ac.uk/

Dik, B. J., Byrne, Z. S., & Steger, M. F. (2013). *Purpose and meaning in the workplace.* American Psychological Association.

Emmons, R. A. (2003). Personal goals, life meaning, and virtue: Wellsprings of a positive life. In C. Keys & J. Haidt (Eds.), *Flourishing: Positive psychology and the well-lived life* (pp. 105–128). American Psychological Association.

Kahn, W. A. (1990). Psychological conditions of personal engagement and disengagement at work. *Academy of Management Journal, 33*, 692–724.

Kahn, W. A. (1992). To be fully there: Psychological presence at work. *Human Relations, 45*, 321–349.

Kahn. W. A., & Fellows, S. (2013). Employee engagement and meaningful work. B. J. Dik, Z. S. Byrne, & M. F. Steger (Eds.), *Purpose and meaning in the workplace*. American Psychological Association.

Kincentric. Retrieved December, 2022, from https://www.kincentric.com/-/media/kincentric/2022/GTEE/Global_Trends_in_Employee_Engagement_2022.pdf

Macey, W. H., & Schneider, B. (2008). The meaning of employee engagement. *Industrial and Organizational Psychology: Perspectives on Science and Practice, 1*, 3–30.

MacLeod Report. Retrieved August 27, 2022, from https://dera.ioe.ac.uk/id/eprint/1810/1/file52215.pdf

Pratt, M. G., & Ashforth, B. E. (2003). Fostering meaningfulness in work and at work. In K. S. Cameron, J. E. Dutton, & R. E. Quinn (Eds.), *Positive organizational scholarship* (pp. 309–327). Berrett-Koehler.

Roethlisberger, F. J., & Dickson, W. J. (1939). *Management and the worker*. Harvard University Press.

Schaufeli, W., & Buunk, B. (2003). Burnout: An overview of 25 years of research and theorizing. In Schabracq et al., *The handbook of work and health psychology*. John Wiley & Sons. https://www.wilmarschaufeli.nl/publications/Schaufeli/181.pdf

Steger, M. F. (in press). Experiencing meaning in life: Optimal functioning at the nexus of spirituality, psychopathology, and well-being. In P. T. P. Wong & P. S. Fry (Eds.), *The human quest for meaning* (2nd ed.). Lawrence Erlbaum.

Steger, M. F. & Dik, B. J. (in press). Work as meaning. In P. A. Linley, S. Harrington & N. Page (Eds.), *Oxford handbook of positive psychology and work*. Oxford University Press.

Steger, M. F., Kashdan, T. B., Sullivan, B. A., & Lorentz, D. (2008). Understanding the search for meaning in life: Personality, cognitive style and the dynamic between seeking and experiencing meaning. *Journal of Personality, 76,* 199–228.

Shoobridge, G. Retrieved November 8, 2022, from https://www.linkedin.com/pulse/employee-engagement-vs-satisfaction-gonzalo-shoobridge

Talk Freely. Retrieved August 22, 2022, from https://www.talkfreely.com/blog/what-is-employee-engagement

Wong, P. T. P. (1998). Spirituality, meaning, and successful aging. In P. T. P. Wong & P. S. Fry (Eds.), *The human quest for meaning: A handbook of psychological research and clinical applications* (pp. 359–394). Lawrence Erlbaum.

Wong, P. T. P. (2011). Positive psychology 2.0: Towards a balanced interactive model of the good life. *Canadian Psychology, 52*(2), 69–81.

Chapter 8: Positive Psychology in Organizations

Bandura, A. (1997). *Self-efficacy: The exercise of control.* Freeman.

Baumeister, R. F., & Vohs, K.D. (2002). The pursuit of meaningfulness in life. In C. R. Snyder & S. J. Lopez (Eds.), *Handbook of positive psychology* (pp. 608–618). Oxford University Press.

Bonaiuto, M., Mao, Y., Roberts, S., Psalti, A., Ariccio, S., Ganucci Cancellieri, U., & Csikszentmihalyi, M. (2016). Optimal experience and personal growth: Flow and the consolidation of place identity. *Frontiers in Psychology, 7,* 1654.

Bonebright, C. A., Clay, D. L., & Ankenmann, R. D. (2000). The relationship of workaholism with work-life conflict, life satisfaction, and purpose in life. *Journal of Counseling Psychology, 47,* 469–477.

Buckinghamshire Five Ways Resource Pack. (2008). Retrieved September 1, 2022, from http://www.bucks.ac.uk/

Buckinghamshire Five Ways Toolkit. (2008). Retrieved September 1, 2022, from http://www.bucks.ac.uk/

Butler, J., & Kern, M. L. (2015). The PERMA-Profiler: A brief multidimensional measure of flourishing. Retrieved November 15, 2022, from http://www.peggykern.org/questionnaires.html

Cameron, K., Mora, C., Leutscher, T., & Calarco, M. (2011). Effects of positive practices of organizational effectiveness. *The Journal of Applied Behavioral Science, 47*(3), 266–308.

CBRE. (2014). Fast Forwards 2030: The future of work and the workplace. Retrieved August 10, 2022, from https://psycnet.apa.org/record/2017-09749-011

Cohn, M. A. & Fredrickson, B.L. (2009). Positive emotions. In *The Oxford handbook of positive psychology* (Second Edition) (pp. 13–24). Oxford University Press.

Cohn, M. A., & Fredrickson, B. L., et al. (2009). Happiness unpacked: Positive emotions increase life satisfaction by building resilience. *Emotion, 9,* 361–386.

Cooperrider, D., & Srivastva, S. (1987). Appreciative inquiry in organizational life. In *Research in organizational change and development* (pp. 81–142). Emerald Publishing Limited.

Csikszentmihalyi, M. (1990). *Flow: The psychology of the optimal experience.* Harper & Row.

Csikszentmihalyi, M. (1996). *Creativity: Flow and the psychology of the discovery and invention.* Harper Perennial.

Deci, E. L., & Ryan, R. M. (1985). *Intrinsic motivation and self-determination in human behavior.* Plenum Press.

Deci, E. L., & Ryan, R. M. (1991). A motivational approach to self: Integration in personality. In R. Dienstbier (Ed.), *Nebraska Symposium on motivation* (vol. 38, pp. 237–288). University of Nebraska Press.

Dutton, J. E., & Heaphy, E. D. (2003). The power of high-quality connections. In K. S. Cameron, J. E. Dutton, & R. E. Quinn (Eds.), *Positive organizational scholarship: Foundations of a new discipline* (pp. 263–278). Berrett-Koehler.

Fredrickson, B. L. (1998). What good are positive emotions? *Review of General Psychology, 2,* 300–319.

Fredrickson, B. (2005). Positive emotions. In C. R. Snyder & S. J. Lopez (Eds.), *Handbook of positive psychology.* Oxford University Press.

Fredrickson, B. (2009). *Positivity* (1st ed.). One World.

Froman, L. (2010). Positive psychology in the workplace. *Journal of Adult Development, 17,* 59069.

Green, S., Evans, O., Williams, B. (2017). Positive psychology at work: Research and practice. In C. Proctor, *Positive psychology interventions in practice* (pp. 185–206). Springer International Publishing.

Ivtzan, I., et al. (2016). *Second wave positive psychology: Embracing the dark side of life.* Routledge.

Lewis, S. (2011). *Positive psychology at work.* Wiley & Sons Ltd.

Linley, A. (2008). *Average to A: Realising strengths in yourself and others.* CAPP.

Luthans, F., Avey, J. B., Avolio, B. J., Norman, S. M., & Combs, G. M. (2006). Psychological capital development: Toward a micro-intervention. *Journal of Organizational Behavior, 27,* 387–393.

Luthans, F., Luthans, K. W., & Luthans, B. C. (2004). *Positive psychological capital: Beyond human and social capital.* Management Department Faculty Publications, 145.

Luthans, F., & Youssef, C. M. (2007). Emerging positive organizational behavior. *Journal of Management, 33,* 321–349.

Luthans, F., & Youssef, C. M. (2011). Positive Workplaces. In S. Lopez & C. R. Snyder, *The Oxford handbook of positive psychology* (pp. 579–588). Oxford University Press.

Macey, W. H., & Schneider, B. (2008). The meaning of employee engagement. *Industrial and Organizational Psychology: Perspectives on Science and Practice, 1,* 3–30.

Masten, A. S. (2001). Ordinary magic: Resilience process in development. *American Psychologist, 56,* 227–239.

McQuaid, M., & Lawn, E. (2014). *Your strengths blueprint: How to be engaged, energized, and happy at work.* Michelle McQuaid Pty Ltd. Also available and last accessed on January 14, 2022, from https:// www.michellemcquaid.com/product/your-strengths-blueprint/

Owens, B., Baker, W., Sumpter, D., & Cameron, K. (2015). Relational energy at work: Implications for job engagement and job performance. *The Journal of Applied Psychology, 101*(1), 35–49.

Parks, A. C., & Biswas-Diener, R. (2013). Positive interventions: Past, present and future. In T. Kashdan & J. Ciarrochi (Eds.), *Mindfulness, acceptance, and positive psychology: The seven foundations of well-being* (pp. 140–165). Context Press.

Peterson, C. (2006). *A primer in positive psychology.* Oxford University Press.

Proctor, C. (2017). *Positive psychology interventions in practice*. Springer International Publishing.

Seligman, M. E. P. (2011). *Flourish: A visionary new understanding of happiness and well-being*. Free Press.

Snyder, C. R. (2000). *Handbook of hope: Theory, measures, and applications*. Academic Press.

Stavros, J., Cooperrider, D., & Kelley, L. (2003). Strategic inquiry with appreciative intent: Inspiration to SOAR!. *AI Practitioner: International Journal of Appreciative Inquiry, 5,* 10–17. Also available from https://www.researchgate.net/publication/285057032_Strategic_inquiry_with_appreciative_intent_Inspiration_to_SOAR

Chapter 9: Internal Communication

All Things IC. Retrieved December 18, 2022, from https://www.allthingsic.com/

Innovisor. Retrieved October 12, 2021, from https://www.innovisor.com/2020/07/08/the-three-percent-rule-your-secret-weapon-for-success-with-change/

Talk Freely. Retrieved March 2, 2023, from https://www.talkfreely.com/download/everything-you-need-to-know-about-internal-communication

The Grossman Group. Retrieved July 1, 2023, from https://www.yourthoughtpartner.com/

Shoobridge, G. Retrieved March 7, 2023, from https://www.linkedin.com/pulse/signs-your-workplace-stuck-communication-limbo-dr-gonzalo-shoobridge

Yeomans, L., & FitzPatrick, L. (2017). Internal communication. In *Exploring public relations*. Pearson Education. Accessed through Beckett Repository record on October 5, 2022: https://eprints.leedsbeckett.ac.uk/id/eprint/3499/

Chapter 10: Motivation, Pride, and Rewards and Recognition

Barrett Values Centre. Retrieved October 10, 2022, from https://www.valuescentre.com

Baumeister, R. F., & Leary, M. R. (1995). The need to belong: Desire for interpersonal attachment as a fundamental human motivation. *Psychological Bulletin, 117,* 497–529.

Burton, K. (2012). A study of motivation: How to get your employees moving. *Management, 3*(2), 232–234.

Day, H. I. (1981). *'Play.' Advances in intrinsic motivation and aesthetics* (pp. 225–250). Plenum Press.

Employee Experience Magazine. Retrieved May 27, 2023, from https://www.emexmag.com/pride-the-unheralded-driver-of-engagement/

Skinner, B. F. (1953). *Science and human behavior.* SimonandSchuster.com.

Ganta, V. C. (2014). Motivation in the workplace to improve the employee performance. *International Journal of Engineering Technology, Management and Applied Sciences, 2*(6), 221–230.

Herzberg, F., Mausner, B., & Snyderman, B. B. (1959). *The motivation to work.* Wiley.

Maslow, A. H. (1943). A theory of human motivation. *Psychological Review, 50,* 370–396.

Barrett, R. (2013). *The values-driven organization: Unleashing human potential for performance and profit.* Routledge. Retrieved March 25, 2021, from http://www.valuescentre.com

Simply Psychology. Retrieved May 8, 2023, from https://www.simplypsychology.org/maslow.html

Your Coach. Retrieved May 7, 2023, from https://www.yourcoach.be/en/employee-motivation-theories/hackman-and-oldham-job-characteristics-model/

Chapter 11: Employees Want Wellbeing From Their Jobs, and They May Resign To Find It

Bend Chamber of Commerce. Retrieved August 5, 2021, from https://bendchamber.org/wp-content/uploads/2021/12/state-of-the-global-workplace-2021-download.pdf

Diener, E., & Biswas Diener, R. (2008). *Happiness: Unlocking the mysteries of psychological wealth.* Oxford.

Deci, E. L., & Ryan, R. M. (2004). *Handbook of self-determination research.* University of Rochester Press.

Deci, E., Koestner, R., & Ryan, R. (2001). Extrinsic rewards and intrinsic motivations in education: Reconsidered once again. *Review of Educational Research, 71*(1), 1–27.

Gallup. Retrieved August 8, 2021, from https://www.gallup.com/workplace/352952/employees-wellbeing-job-leave-find.aspx

Gallup. Retrieved July 17, 2023, from https://www.gallup.com/workplace/349484/state-of-the-global-workplace.aspx

IWBI: WELL. Retrieved July 7, 2023, from https://www.wellcertified.com/

Microsoft. Retrieved August 30, 2021, from https://www.microsoft.com/en-us/worklab/work-trend-index/hybrid-work

Nakamura, J., & Csikszentmihalyi, M. (2002). The concept of flow. In C. R. Snyder & S. J. Lopez (Eds.), *Handbook of positive psychology* (pp. 89–105). Oxford University Press.

Nakamura, J., & Csikszentmihalyi, M. (2009). Flow theory and research. In C. R. Snyder & S. J. Lopez (Eds.), *Handbook of positive psychology* (pp. 195–206). Oxford University Press.

Ryff, C. D. (1989). Happiness is everything, or is it? Exploration of the meaning of psychological well-being. *Journal of Personality and Social Psychology, 57,* 1069–1081.

Ryff, C. D., & Keys, C. L. M. (1995). The structure of psychological well-being revisited. *Journal of Personality and Social Psychology, 69*(4), 719–727.

Chapter 12: Learning and Performance

Dewey J. (1933). *How we think.* D. C. Heath and Co.

Dewey, J. (1944). *Democracy and education.* Free Press. Original work published 1916.

Fanning, R. M., & Gaga, D. M. (2007). The role of debriefing in simulation-based learning. *Society for Simulation in Healthcare, 2*(2).

Fredrickson, B. L. (1998). What good are positive emotions? *Review of General Psychology, 2,* 300–319.

Harvard Business Review. Retrieved July 29, 2023, from https://hbr.org/2016/10/the-performance-management-revolution

Hidi, S. (1990). Interest and its contribution as a mental resource for learning. *Review of Educational Research, 60*(4), 549–571.

Joy, S., & Kolb, D. A. (2007). *Are there cultural differences in learning style?* Working paper. Department of Organizational Behavior, Case Western Reserve University.

Kolb, D. A., & Fry, R. (1975). Toward an applied theory of experiential learning. In C. Cooper (Ed.), *Theories of Group Process.* John Wiley.

Kolb, D. A. (1984). *Experiential learning: Experience as the source of learning and development* (vol. 1). Prentice-Hall.

Kolb, D., Rubin, I., & Osland, J. (2001). *Organizational behavior: An experiential approach* (7th ed.). Prentice-Hall.

Kolb, A., & Kolb, D. (2010). Learning to play, playing to learn: A case study of a ludic learning space. *Journal of Organizational Change Management, 23*(1), 26–50.

Kolb, D. A., & Kolb, A. (2011). Experiential learning theory: A dynamic, holistic approach to management learning, education and development. In S. J. Armstrong & C. Fukami (Eds.), *Handbook of management learning, education and development ER*. Sage Publications.

Krapp, A. (1999). Interest, motivation and learning: An educational-psychological perspective. *European Journal of Psychology of Education, 14*(1), 23–40.

Lewin, K. (1951). *Field theory in social science: Selected theoretical papers* (edited by Dorwin Cartwright.). Harpers.

Mezirow, J. (1978). Perspective transformation. *Adult Education, 28*, 100–110.

Mezirow, J. (1991). *Transformative dimensions of adult learning*. Jossey-Bass.

Mezirow, J. (1997). Transformative learning: Theory to practice. In P. Cranton (Ed.), Transformative learning in action: Insights from practice. *New Directions for Adult and Continuing Education, 74*, 5–12. Jossey-Bass.

Packer, J. (2004). Motivational factors and the experience of learning in educational leisure settings. Unpublished doctoral dissertation. Queensland University of Technology, Brisbane.

Packer, J., & Ballantyne, R. (2004). Is educational leisure a contradiction in terms: Exploring the synergy of education and entertainment. *Annals of Leisure Research, 7*(1), 54–71.

Roberts, L. (1997). *From knowledge to narrative: Educators and the changing museum*. Smithsonian Institution Press.

Taylor, E. W. (2007). An update of transformative learning theory: A critical review of the empirical research (1999–2005). *International Journal of Lifelong Education, 26*, 173–191.

Training Industry. Retrieved July 30, 2023, from https://trainingindustry. com/wiki/content-development/the-702010-model-for-learning -and-development/

VIA Institute on Character. Retrieved September 2, 2021, from https:// www.viacharacter.org/

Chapter 13: The Exit

McKinsey & Company. Retrieved September 9, 2021, from https:// www.mckinsey.com/capabilities/people-and-organizational- performance/our-insights/great-attrition-or-great-attraction-the- choice-is-yours

Chapter 14: The Metrics Chapter

Academy to Innovate HR. Retrieved February 2, 2022, from https:// www.aihr.com/blog/employer-branding-metrics/

PERMAH. Retrieved October 1, 2021, from https://org.permahsurvey. com/employee_login.php?fp=1

The Vega Factor. Retrieved December 1, 2021, from https://www. vegafactor.com/book

Finnegan Institute. Retrieved October 19, 2021, from https://www. finneganinstitute.com/stay-interviews/

ACKNOWLEDGMENTS

I am deeply indebted to the individuals, teams, and organizations that have been instrumental in my journey of learning and growth, shaping my understanding of the employee experience.

Gerard Moss
You helped me and continue to help me dream. You helped me jump!

Since I first stumbled into the realm of Employee Engagement in the Hospitality industry in 2008, your trust in me, your endless guidance, and the profound sense of purpose you instilled in me have been foundational to my journey. Your wisdom and mentorship have not only contributed significantly to my success but have also allowed me to live out your mantra of "positively impacting people's lives every day." I am forever grateful to you for your kindness and for sharing in the meticulous editing of each chapter of this book. In many ways, the words, thoughts, and sentiments of this book are a reflection of your influence.

My Team

To the passionate individuals who have been with me from the start, both permanent employees on my team and interns, management trainees, cross-trainees, and volunteers who transformed our creative ideas into reality—thank you! I extend my appreciation to all the managers and senior leaders across various organizations who supported and nurtured my vision, allowing it to surpass my wildest dreams. A heartfelt thankyou to all the business partners who have collaborated and continue to partner with me on all my projects. You guys are phenomenal!

My Friends

You know who you are, and the list is too extensive to enumerate here. I am immensely grateful for your presence, trust, words of encouragement, and feedback. To my talented designers, photographers, and illustrators—your artistry will endure within and beyond this book.

My Family

My mother, Madlena Minkovska, your ambitious vision for me has been a guiding force throughout my life. Thank you for raising me as 'a free-range chicken,' as per your words, and for fostering the creative freedom that shapes the person I am today.

To my late father, George Vanev, may your soul rest in peace. Your legacy of kindness, generosity, and curiosity continues to inspire me and shape my values in life.

To my grandparents, Mama Poli and Dedi, who helped to raise me—your influence is ingrained in me, and I see so much of you in me. And I know you see it, too. I know you are proud of this book.

To my intelligent husband, Mounaim Lamouni, you motivate me to be a better person every single day.

To each of you who have played a priceless role in my life and, by extension, in the lives of those touched by my endeavors—Blagodaria ("thank you" in Bulgarian)!

AUTHOR BIO

Kristina Vaneva is a celebrated HR industry leader who has garnered numerous accolades and industry awards for her remarkable contributions to the field of employee experience. With an impressive career journey spanning over two decades, specializing in employee engagement and internal communication, Kristina's mission is to foster hope, positivity, and happiness in workplaces and individuals' lives.

Kristina is esteemed for her ability to drive employee engagement and happiness, reduce employee turnover rates and turnover costs, and seize opportunities for positive organizational change. She is a devoted leader with a proven track record of crafting impactful communication strategies tailored to business objectives. Her unique talent lies in creating innovative rewards, memorable recognition programs, and incredible social events that elevate the employee experience.

Kristina's strength lies in initiating transformative organizational changes and implementing measurable strategies.

In addition to her Bachelor of Communications, Kristina's academic journey includes a Master of Science in Applied

Positive Psychology and a Master of Business Administration in Telecommunications.

Beyond her professional pursuits, she enjoys spending time with her family and friends, scuba diving, dragon boating, cycling, nature walks, reading, traveling, exploring art galleries, and solving exhilarating escape room challenges.

Notes

....

....

....

....

....

....

....

....

....

....

....

....

....

....

www.ingramcontent.com/pod-product-compliance
Lightning Source LLC
Chambersburg PA
CBHW030452210326
41597CB00013B/637